God's Signature

God's Signature

The Wonders of the Hebrew Scriptures

Steve Maltz

*Terra*Nova
PUBLICATIONS

Published in Great Britain by
Terra Nova Publications International Ltd.
PO Box 2400 Bradford-on-Avon BA15 2YN

Cover design by Phil Maltz

978–0–9570473–0–3

Printed in Great Britain

Contents

Acknowledgements

This book took me way out of my comfort zone, so many, many thanks to the people who treated me gently with their comments and observations. From the great biblical minds that are David Pawson and Chris Hill, to the expert eyes of John Smith and Robin Eastwood, the wisdom of Kit Eglinton and Peter Sammons, the critical eye of Jackie Stratton, the eagerness and encouragement of Peter Byron-Davies, but last – and definitely *not* least – to Monica, my best mate, unafraid to criticise (as is her right), but bursting with support and enthusiasm.

Introduction

Prepare to embark on an exciting journey ... into the very heart of God.

Hold on, hold on, where are you taking me?

You may want to go on this journey, or something may be holding you back. Do you really trust the driver? *Is he qualified to take passengers and, if so, who says so?* After all, we are dealing with a period of history that we don't have complete certainty about, this world of early Bible times. We have biblical scholars today with all sorts of opinions as to how the Hebrew Scriptures, the "Old Testament", came to be written and compiled. Every opinion should have a post-it note attached, reminding us as to how this scholar reached his or her conclusion. This is more important than you may think and you may be sorely tempted to slam on the brakes now. For that reason you need to know a bit about this driver.

When we make the assertion that the Bible is the Word of God, what do we actually mean? Do we mean that the Bible *contains* the Word of God, among other stuff and that *some* of this "other stuff" may be a bit iffy – *because that's what some scholars have been telling us*? Or do we mean that the Bible is, in total, the absolute, complete Word of God, down to the last jot and tittle? Or is there some point in-between these positions that we can live with?

Here is where I'm coming from. I believe that everything, from the big ideas to the little squiggles in God's Word to mankind are relevant, instructional and have been put there by the divine will for a divine purpose. This is not an empty assertion because the whole point of this book is to provide a good case for my belief. We are going to places few have dared explore, because most have no idea these places exist and haven't been given the tools to get there. You are going to gain a whole new layer of understanding of our wonderful God and his wonderful Book through our exploration of his wonderful language, Hebrew. You will do this through two journeys.

Firstly, the journey *of* God's Word, where we are going to see how the Hebrew Scriptures were breathed out from God onto the pages of our Bibles. We are going to find out why God chose this strange (to our eyes) language of Hebrew anyway and, by the time you finish reading, you will find yourself marvelling at this wonderful language and exclaiming: *How could he not have chosen it?* You will be introduced to the origins, development and basic grammar of Hebrew along the way as we explore how God used it to create his Scriptures, from his finger, to Moses' endeavours, right through to the work of Ezra the scribe.

Meshing together historical narratives with simple Hebrew word studies, we will follow through the story of how the "Old Testament" canon was set and how God's Word was translated into other languages – first Greek, Latin and then English. We will follow the activities of Ezra and the early scribes, as they meticulously copied the Hebrew Scriptures from generation to generation, paying particular attention to the highly influential Masoretes, whose work still resonates through every version of the "Old Testament" you will read. We will examine these men and their work and ponder on their legacy before rummaging through the pages of some popular English translations of the Hebrew Scriptures, looking at the good and bad points.

The second journey is *within* God's Word, where we see how the Hebrew Scriptures breathe life into our understanding of God and his ways. Using the basic knowledge of Hebrew that we gained from Part One, we are going to meander through a series of Hebrew Word Studies. We are going to see what has been lost to those of us who have to rely on an English translation to read from God's Word. We are going to allow the original Hebrew Scriptures to speak to us in a way that English is just not equipped to do, both because of the inadequacies of the alphabet and language and the shortcomings or agendas of the English translators.

These Hebrew Word Studies are not only there to show us what we've been missing but they are going to give us great insights into how God sees us and his creation, and how he has sprinkled knowledge of his coming Messiah all through the words of Holy Scripture. We are also going to be introduced to that intriguing and complex method of Jewish Bible study, the *Midrash*. Then we are going to read about a real-life detective story involving the Hebrew Scriptures and their translations, taking us through many of the areas that we have covered in this book (if you have been paying attention!)

Finally we are left to ponder the very heart of the material presented here: where is *God's Signature* and how can we read it and act on it? So sit back, polish your (physical and spiritual) spectacles and get ready for a fascinating journey.

Part One
The Journey of God's Word

Chapter One

Hebrew and the Hebraic

I will start with a single, simple statement: *The Bible is God's Word to us.* You either believe this, or you *really* believe this. If you *really* believe this then you consider the Bible so precious that every time someone prods it with a stick, it hurts ... it *really* hurts, just as it must hurt God Himself.

And when I say "prod it with a stick", it's the *proverbial* stick I am talking about. It goes by the name of *textual criticism* and really got going in Europe in the sixteenth century, when the "rational" mind had taken over from the heart of faith, in matters of religion. It caused us to start to ask questions like these:

- Who wrote the Bible, human beings or God?
- Is there any error in the Bible and, if so, is it important?
- How do we trace the manuscript evidence for the Bible?
- Who decided what material to include in the Bible?

It may seem to be a worthy exercise, getting to grips with the authorship, veracity and timeline of the Bible, but it can also seem like doing an autopsy on a living body! That's the point, really. The Bible is no dead tome, it is vibrantly alive, as is its Author. It is like no other book, *it is God's Word to us*, so we must treat it as a treasured, precious gem.

I'm not purposely being anti-intellectual, irrational and naive, but the process of textual criticism intends to increase our knowledge of a piece of literature, with the understanding that it's a continual process, feeding from archaeological finds and new research and therefore needing constant analysis and re-analysis.

But this is God's Word that's the issue here. I reject textual criticism as the primary tool for an understanding of the Bible because I have perfect 100% faith that God just wants us to believe that *it is what he tells us it is.* The Bible defines itself here in broad terms:

> *All Scripture is God-breathed and is useful for teaching, rebuking, correcting and training in righteousness, so that the man of God may be thoroughly equipped for every good work* (2 Timothy 3:16–17).

What this says to me is that God breathed his words to us in some way and our job is to figure out what those words were. We need to do so because otherwise we're not equipped for the work he has for us. So we need those words, from God's heart to our own. No easy task, made harder by the realities of entropy and the fiasco at Babel. *What a strange sentence!* "Entropy" is the scientific observation that all things decay, including scrolls and parchments of God's words, and the Babel thing (see Genesis 11) gave us the confusion of languages, necessitating translations of God's words. Working together, this means that we no longer have access to those first words in a language we can understand. Short of entering a time capsule and whisking ourselves off to the days of Moses, how do we know that God's Word is the same yesterday, today and forever? Are we reading Scripture as originally intended? It is the purpose of this book to get as close as we can to those God-breathed words.

As I have said umpteen times in my recent books, when it comes to looking at the ways of man, there are only two mindsets to consider, the *Greek* one and the *Hebraic* one. Now *textual criticism* is very much a result of Greek thinking. This is not to reject it entirely, but to put it in its rightful place, as a tool to show us *how* God did it, rather than to ask *whether* God did it, adding doubt and confusion.

Greek thinking analyses the various components of the Hebrew Scriptures, declaring them, as a product of human effort at a point in time, to be analysed and compared to other documents produced in other places and at other times. It creates analytical tools and techniques to aid this process such as eclecticism, stemmatics and cladistics, whatever *they* are! It also gives rise to other methodologies, such as source criticism, form criticism and redaction criticism, whatever they are! (For an introduction to the Greek mindset I refer you to my earlier book *How the Church Lost the Truth*.)

They are all tools to prod away, whether as a chisel or as a sledgehammer, but often with the end product of chipping away at the very foundations of our faith, the Word of God. Rather than being sucked into such distractions we would be better employed actually reading the Word of God, believing it and doing what it says!

By contrast, Hebraic thinking looks at the Author himself and decides that the best way to get to know him is to read what he has to say. It's as simple as that, and if you're intrigued enough to want to know more about the Hebraic mindset, then do have a look at my book entitled *To Life!*

As we move forwards in our journey, we will continue in the Hebraic mindset that the Bible is God's Word to us and allow the Holy Spirit and the Book itself to guide us. But before we do so, we go backwards, to a time long, long ago. ...

If you were God and wished to communicate your innermost thoughts to your people in the simplest way, what would you do? Of course you would talk to some key people, the movers and shakers whom you could trust to get the word out. There was Adam, the first man, with whom you walked and talked. Then there were Abraham and Moses. You talked to both of them and cut covenants with them on behalf of their people. You knew that you could trust these men to convey your words to others, but you also knew that a time would come when a more permanent, universal way would need to be found to *really* get the message out.

They already had a language that lasted them from Eden to Babel, a single tongue that made it easy for you to communicate with them, and them with each other. But then, of course, they messed things up at the *Tower of Babel* and needed to be taken down a peg or two, so you confused their language and sent them packing far and wide.

Of all the people around at that time, you had your eye on one group, the *Semites*, headed by Abram and his clans. They were the ones you wanted to really communicate with, so you made sure their language was going to be the very best to convey your thoughts to the minds and hearts of mankind. And you were going to make very sure that this language would be easily understood in written form, in a very special way. This was to be a very special language, probably related to the same language you taught to Adam in the Garden of Eden. This language was *Hebrew*.

For God to choose (or create) Hebrew as his primary means of communicating to mankind, there had to be some unique features that marked it out as fit for purpose. Indeed there *are* and, rather than my telling you now, you will find out for yourself as the story unfolds.

Now imagine you are a shepherd travelling with Abram from Haran to Canaan. Of course, "shepherd" was not the actual word they would have used for you. They would have used this Hebrew word:

רֹעֶה *(ro'eh)*

As you can see, this is made up of three letters (reading from right to left), *resh* (ר) – *ayin* (ע) – *hey* (ה). On a plaque outside your tent you proudly display your title *ro'eh*. It wouldn't be using those exact Hebrew letters, though, but rather an earlier form of them. It's time for a short lesson on the history of writing.

It all started with pictures. If you wanted to express yourself (other than through speech, of course), you drew a picture. Perhaps you killed a wild beast, or your tent burnt down, or you spotted an enemy encampment. You drew a picture to represent what you were seeing or thinking. It would have been a crude drawing, just a few scratches on clay perhaps – you would hardly have access to oil paints and a canvas would you?

This was quite a limited situation. It would have been fine if you could draw pictures of everything you wanted to express, but people had neither the time nor the imagination to take it that far. Instead they combined pictures to make up words. In a sense, we had the start of an alphabet here. A small number of key pictures – such as an eye, a tent or an ox – were simplified and turned into letters, and the sound of what was depicted in the picture developed into the sound of the letter. This is simpler than I have described and an example is needed. Let's go back to the shepherd.

The Hebrew word, *ro'eh*, is written as רֹעֶה in modern Hebrew, with those three letters, *resh* (ר), *ayin* (ע) and *hey* (ה), reading from right to left. Each of those three letters developed over time from earlier forms – in fact each was originally a *picture*.

Hebrew is basically a language formed from pictures. We are going back to well before the time of Moses. The alphabet that had developed, one of the earliest in the world, is called by scholars the *Proto-Canaanite alphabet*. Here's the first picture in our word, in that alphabet:

It's plain to see that this is a picture of a head, a man's head.

Here's the second picture:

This is not quite so obvious. It's a picture of an eye. And here's the final picture:

It's a man with his arms lifted up. He's looking at something, or showing or revealing something.

The word for "shepherd" was made by putting these three pictures or *letters* together (reading from right to left).

It doesn't make sense until we use our imagination and think of a man (depicted by his head), looking (depicted by an eye) in a purposeful fashion (depicted by outstretched arms). This sort of describes what a shepherd does! It may not be neat and tidy and exact, but they didn't have our twenty-first century sophistication and logical minds. That's the essence of *Hebrew*, and the *Hebraic mind*, as we shall see again and again in this book. It's a way of looking at the world in a general, fuzzy and forgiving way and thinking such thoughts as, *hmm ... man looks out in an important way ... that could mean a few things, but I can see a shepherd doing that ... yes, those three marks I have just made on clay mean shepherd to me, let's go and tell others. ...*

The "Greek" mind would see this in a different way. It would ponder over those three symbols and create a discussion with others over it and just agonise for ages, like this: *there are so many different ways these pictures can be interpreted; it's just not clear and exact enough for me. We need a set of symbols that just shout out "shepherd" and nothing else. ...*

Interestingly, this Hebrew word can also be translated as *pastor*, which probably fits the pictures even better!

Time moved on and the early Hebrew language, which scholars call *Phoenician-Old Hebrew*, developed from this cruder Proto-Canaanite form. The letters started to change – into a form that more resembles what letters are meant to look like to our modern eye.

ヨ O ᐸ

Then, at around the time of the Babylonian exile, the letters again changed, into the form that is the basis for the Hebrew in our written Scriptures. Quite a jump really and it probably didn't happen overnight, but in incremental stages.

רעה

And this is *ro'eh*, the Hebrew name for shepherd. We will talk about the right-to-left business a bit later on, as well as the fact that vowels haven't come into the picture yet (though we are including them in our pronunciations, otherwise it would all sound a bit rasping, guttural or just plain Klingon!), but suffice to say we will discover that many words that we find in the "Old Testament" will be constructed initially from pictures.

Let's just think about that for a moment. When we look at the English word *shepherd* we get no *visual* clues from the individual letters about the meaning of the word. Hebrew is a very visual language, so much so that we can make the following statement:

Question: Why did God choose Hebrew?
Answer #1: Because letters can often add a visual meaning.

Here's another example. Look at the following "word pictures":

This is a word written in the original proto-Canaanite alphabet. Let's take each letter in turn, reading from right to left. The first signifies a *door*, the second a *house* and the third a *head* (we've already seen this one). The gist is to **find a doorway into the house of a person**, i.e. a pathway into a person's mind.

This developed into the *Phoenician-Old Hebrew* language, becoming:

⟨ ⟩

And then into Biblical Hebrew:

דבר

This is the word *davar*, Hebrew for "word", a *pathway into a person's mind*, if you think about it.

Hebrew is more interesting than we thought, eh?

Chapter Two

Moses has an Encounter

This is what we're going to do. We are going to allow the Bible to be our guide in the first instance. We are going to allow it to tell its own story. The first thing it is going to tell us is how it first came to be written. We turn to the book *Exodus*.

Moses has led the Israelite nation out of Egyptian bondage on the night of the *Passover*. It is going to be seven weeks before they reach Mount Sinai. This period of time is known as the *omer* and it takes us to the next great biblical feast, that of *Shavuot* (known to you as "Pentecost"), the Feast of Weeks.

While the impatient and unruly ex-slaves stand around fidgeting, Moses climbs the mountain for a forty day one-to-one with God himself. Now forty days is a long time. For the people of Israel, waiting for Moses at the foot of Sinai, it is getting hotter, hotter, hotter and they are getting more and more impatient. Eventually he comes down and … oh dear! They have built a golden calf and are offering sacrifices to it. God is most displeased and offers to blot them out and start building up a new people from Moses' family. Moses does not take up this offer and reminds God of the great investment he has made in these Israelites, urging him to continue with the line of Abraham, Isaac and Jacob. These are verses worth re-reading for those who believe that prayer can't change situations!

What does Moses do? He *schleps* his eighty year-old bones back up Mount Sinai for another forty days and nights. What had happened in those (two sets of) forty days and nights was the first step in the story of the Bible. The first words written are immortalised in Exodus 20. Contrary to popular thought, they are *not* called the "Ten Commandments", but rather the *Ten Words, aseret ha-devarim* in Hebrew.

And God spoke all these words:

> "I am the LORD your God, who brought you out of Egypt, out of the land of slavery.
>
> "You shall have no other gods before me.
>
> "You shall not make for yourself an idol in the form of anything in heaven above or on the earth beneath or in the waters below. You shall not bow down to them or worship them; for I, the LORD your God, am a jealous God, punishing the children for the sin of the fathers to the third and fourth generation of those who hate me, but showing love to a thousand [generations] of those who love me and keep my commandments.
>
> "You shall not misuse the name of the LORD your God, for the LORD will not hold anyone guiltless who misuses his name.
>
> "Remember the Sabbath day by keeping it holy. Six days you shall labour and do all your work, but the seventh day is a Sabbath to the LORD your God. On it you shall not do any work, neither you, nor your son or daughter, nor your manservant or maidservant, nor your animals, nor the alien within your gates. For in six days the LORD made the heavens and the earth, the sea, and all that is in them, but he rested on the seventh day. Therefore the LORD blessed the Sabbath day and made it holy.
>
> "Honour your father and your mother, so that you may live long in the land the LORD your God is giving you.
>
> "You shall not murder.
>
> "You shall not commit adultery.
>
> "You shall not steal.
>
> "You shall not give false testimony against your neighbour.
>
> "You shall not covet your neighbour's house. You shall not covet your neighbour's wife, or his manservant or maidservant, his ox or donkey, or anything that belongs to your neighbour" *(Exodus 20:1–17).*

Those 228 words were written in Old Hebrew script, by the very finger of God.

When the LORD *finished speaking to Moses on Mount Sinai, he gave him the two tablets of the Testimony, the tablets of stone inscribed by the finger of God* (Exodus 31:18).

So God got things moving himself. The first words in the Bible were his own, written on two tablets of stone, the "Ten Words", the *testimony* of God.

This is where the "Greek mind" and the "Hebrew mind" very much part company. The Hebraic mind has room for the miraculous intervention of God in the affairs of man and accepts the plain words of the narrative. If God wanted to use his finger to inscribe these words, and has troubled to tell us this, what right do we have to doubt him?

The discussions that the rabbis of old had were concerned with the *actual writing* on the tablets – whether each tablet had five "commandments" and whether the letters were etched right through the stone, so that they could be read from both sides. They had absolutely no doubts as to how the words got there, they were content to take God's word for it.

The *Greek* mind would approach things in a very different way. The *documentary hypothesis,* devised in the nineteenth century, would declare that the "Ten Commandments" would have been written by a human, the "so-called" *Yahwist* writer living in the kingdom of Judah in the ninth century BC, and could have been modelled on the writings of the Hittites and other peoples living in Mesopotamia at an earlier time. There are many different theories of this ilk, and more will undoubtedly appear in the future as academic biblical scholarship ventures relentlessly forwards. For these people the Bible is not to be trusted alone to verify itself but should be analysed in much the same way as any other book would be.

But these are God's Words, the precious Words of our Creator; can't we take his Word seriously? The only mitigating circumstance could be that we are not totally sure that the words of the Bible we read today are, for whatever reason, the words that were originally written. This concern is going to be addressed as we continue our story in this book.

One may argue that the rabbis of old who pondered such things as these tablets of stone were not believers in Jesus and so should be ignored. Yet they never doubted that God indeed *was* the author of the Ten Commandments, unlike Julius Wellhausen, formulator of the "documentary hypothesis", who was a Lutheran and so would claim to be a believer, yet had *no* doubts that God *wasn't* the author of the Ten Commandments.

Now answer this: *Who did more for the glory of God?* We should not be quick to judge according to our prejudices or inclinations, and we should assess teachings by their consequences, as long as these teachings do not contradict the revelation given to us by the life and ministry of Jesus Christ.

One of the words carved out by the finger of God would have been his very name, as announced right at the start of the Ten Commandments.

"*I am the* LORD *your God*" (Exodus 20:2a).

We will revisit this simple statement a few times in this book and we'll see it as a sign of our developing understanding of God's communication to man. The Hebrew words for this phrase are:

אנכי יהוה אלהיך

Reading from right to left, the first letter of this key biblical phrase, *the first letter written by God to mankind*, is this one:

א

It's the *aleph*, the first letter of the Hebrew alphabet. The Bible is full of such significances, as we shall see as we go deeper. There is a danger, though, of going overboard on significances, because there is a mystical tradition attached to the Hebrew alphabet that may be very enticing and interesting. We must not allow ourselves to be tickled by anything outside of God's revealed Word.

> *For the time will come when men will not put up with sound doctrine. Instead, to suit their own desires, they will gather*

> *around them a great number of teachers to say what their*
> *itching ears want to hear* (2 Timothy 4:3).

So we must not scratch our itching ears with any of the utterances from the Zohar, the chief sourcebook for the *Kabbalah*. Other things, such as *Gematria*, giving significance to numerical equivalents of the Hebrew letters, are borderline, and you should tread warily, as the devil has a counterfeit called *numerology*, which could take you into areas best left alone.

Then there are the ideas circulating about so-called Bible codes. Oy! Very enticing, very interesting and I don't wish to pass judgement on this, except to say that it has certainly been abused by some, who appear to have seen this area as giving apparent licence for what is basically fortune telling.

My gut instinct is to stick by the assertion that the Word of God in the Bible should be in plain sight, even though truths must sometimes be coaxed out of it. Bible "codes" are hidden, even esoteric, not easily accessible to anyone except the few. This smacks of *gnosticism*, a very pervasive heresy that claims that some people have *special knowledge*, thus giving them a hold over others. This ain't kosher!

When you see a representative picture of the two slabs of the Ten Words (Ten Commandments), the first letter seen is always the א. Actually this is not historically accurate as, at the time of Moses, the earlier form of Hebrew, *Phoenician–Old Hebrew*, was the language *du jour*. Interestingly, Hollywood got it right on this one – almost. In the movie, *The Ten Commandments*, Charlton Heston (Moses) holds up the tablets with Phoenician–Old Hebrew writing on them. The problem is that the words seem to be gobbledegook, and every publicity picture I have seen has different words on the tablets, depending on which way Mr Heston is facing! Hollywood appears to make its own rules!

The *aleph* on Mr Heston's tablet would be this one:

And this would have evolved from the Proto-Canaanite letter picture.

This is a picture of an ox's head and it signified the ideas of leadership or strength. So the aleph (א) too signifies the idea of leadership and strength.

Here are a few examples to illustrate this:

This is the strong leader of the house. This becomes:

אב = aleph bet = *av* = the father, the leader of the house.

This is the strong nail, being nailed to what you allow yourself to desire. This becomes:

אוה = aleph vav hey= *avah* = lust, desire.

This is the strong fence or protector of the house. This becomes:

אח = aleph chet = *ach* = the brother, the protector of the house.

Finally, we have:

The strong water, or nourisher, or lifegiver.

אמ = aleph mem = *em* = the mother, the nourisher.

So you've now got some basic Hebrew words under your belt. Let's move on.

——————————

We will now return to the opening statement of the Ten Commandments:

אנכי יהוה אלהיך "*I am the* LORD *your God*".

We must remind ourselves that these words are just formed of consonants. Vowels haven't yet been discussed. Why? Good question. You probably know (or at least you are going to find out soon) that the Hebrew Scriptures were written *without any vowels*. Why? Good question again. Now for some answers.

English without vowels can be a real stinker of a language. Try making sense of the following: *thsbtsntfrls*. Even with spaces between words it's still a bit of a puzzle: *ths bt s nt fr ls*. With vowels this becomes: *this boat is not for lease*. It could also be: *this bet is not free, also*. Just think, that word *bt* could be: *bet, but, boat, abet, bout, bat, bit, bait, bite, boot, etc.* These words are totally unrelated, and not even the context of the sentence is enough to figure out exactly what is being said.

Hebrew is an interesting language. It *can* live without vowels; it has to really, otherwise the Hebrew Scriptures would be a complete nonsense. The reason it can live without vowels is all down to the way it is constructed. Hebrew words are mostly built around a three letter root, just *three consonants*. From this root can come any number of nouns, as well as verbs, adjectives, adverbs or whatever. And all of these would share a meaning, even if – with our Western, "Greek" eyes – some of these meanings are a little bit tenuous.

This is the beauty of Hebrew. It may look like a mess, it may be written "backwards", but it is beautifully and logically constructed! God really has provided us with a wonderful language by which we can get to know him better. It's a shame that most of us either don't know this, or know it but are put off by the strangeness of it all!

Let's have a look at an example to illustrate this. Here's a familiar word: *Shalom*. It is formed from the three consonants *shin* (שׁ), *lamed* (ל) and *mem* (מ).

שׁלם

Although we tend to take the meaning of *peace*, the word really conveys the ideas of completeness and wholeness.

There are literally hundreds of Hebrew words that have these three letters as their basic root and each of them shares similar meanings. Here are some of them:

Shelem: peace offering.
Shalem: complete.
Shilem: returned to state of completeness.

These three, as sharp eyes will have discovered, are formed from the same three consonants, but with different vowels – which we haven't discussed yet. There are other variations, too, all expressing the idea of harmony, being full, being well, prosperity and being covered.

מושלם *(mem – vav – shin – lamed – mem)* = ***mushlam*** = *perfect.*

As we progress through this book, this is going to be the standard way I'll be using to express Hebrew words. First, the word itself (without vowels), followed by a list of the Hebrew letters used (with bold type used to indicate the sounds of the letters), followed by a transliteration (i.e. written with English letters to show how you say the word), then the English translation. Don't worry about the letters themselves or any grammatical considerations, they will be covered below.

In the above example you can see that our three-letter root is in the last three letters of the word.

להשלים *(lamed – hey – shin – lamed – yod – mem)* = ***lehashlim*** = *to complete, fill in.*
לשלם *(lamed – shin – lamed – mem)* = ***leshalem*** = *to pay.*

תשלום *(tav – shin – lamed – vav – mem)* = **tashlum** = *payment.*
שילומים *(shin – yod – lamed – vav – mem – yod – mem)* = **shi-lumim** = *reparations.*

You can see our three-letter root in all of the above words, though not always in the same place and not always as consecutive letters.

Here's another example. It's a word that you probably use so much that you don't even realise it's a Hebrew word. Amen to that! Yes, you've already been speaking Hebrew every time you finish off a prayer. *Amen*!

אמן *(aleph – mem – nun)* = **amen.**

This three letter root word is also used in two other key words:

אמת *(aleph – mem – tav)* = **emet.**

This means truth, reliability, firmness or trustworthiness.

אמונה *(aleph – mem – vav – nun – hey)* = **emunah.**

This means faithfulness, steadiness, trust.

All three words are bound up in man's relationship to God and are all tied up in God's character, his faithfulness, stability and constancy. Each word takes God's character as a given and has us humans connecting up to him as best we can. *Amen* is our endorsement of God's actions, and the more connected we are to him, the stronger our "amen" will be! It is putting him at the centre and aligning ourselves in orbit around him. All three words are totally God-centred, and the more we claim them for ourselves and our actions, the closer we are in synchronising our will to his. The next time you *amen* a prayer, make sure you mean it. It would be inadvisable to partner with God on false pretences.

What we have learnt so far is that Hebrew can convey meaning not just through the choice of letter but in the combination of letters. This will sink in more and more as we proceed with our story. And, of course, this leads us to ask our question again.

Question: Why did God choose Hebrew?
Answer #2: Because every word can have such a depth of meaning.

Chapter Three
All about *Torah*

So we have two stone tablets inscribed with the Ten Commandments. We remind ourselves of the first three words:

אנכי יהוה אלהיך "*I am the* LORD YOUR GOD"
Elohekha Adonai Anoki

We can see that there are two *alephs* (א) – the one at the beginning of the first word and the one at the start of the third word. The first word, אנכי (*anoki*), takes the meaning "I am", but this very word is mainly used in the context of a *royal* command. Its literal meaning is *Because I am* and it is used over a hundred times in Scripture. It is God himself speaking here and we're not to forget that. It underlines all that follows and puts a divine seal on the proclamations that form the Ten Commandments. These aren't *ordinary* instructions, these are part of God's Word of life for us!

We are now going to look at this third word, or rather, the first *two* letters:

אל

We have already seen the first letter, the *aleph* (א), the letter that evolved from the Proto-Canaanite letter picture:

We remember that this is a picture of an ox's head, signifying the idea of leadership and strength. The other letter is a lamed (ל).

Here is the original Proto-Canaanite letter picture, representing a *staff* or a *crook* and conveying the idea of guiding:

ף

This, in turn, transformed into the *Phoenician – Old Hebrew* letter:

ᒪ

So, the original word gives the sense of "strong guided leadership". The modern pronunciation of **אל** is **el** and it is the generic title for *God*. This is a good fit to the original meaning of those letters. It is not the *personal* name of God (more of that later) but it is a word that appears all over the Hebrew Scriptures, sometimes as a prefix or suffix.

Here's our phrase again:

אנכי יהוה אלהיך "*I am the* LORD *your* GOD."

The word **אלהיך** translates as *"your God"*, formed from two parts: **ך** (your) and **אלהים** (God).

Now God has many names, each expressing a facet of his character. Here's one of them:

אל שדי *(aleph – lamed shin – dalet – yod)* = *el shaday*

Most Jewish and Christian Bibles translate this as "God Almighty", but that doesn't tell the full story. Actually it's quite an earthy one, so, if you're easily shocked, cover your eyes now!

Let's look at the root of *shaday:*

שד

Let's see what Proto-Canaanite letter pictures this developed from:

The first letter (reading from right to left) is a *shin* and the picture is of the two front teeth, or of just two.... Well, it needs to be seen in conjunction with the other letter, the *dalet*, which can be a door, or something that hangs down, like a shutter. The overall impression of the root word of *shaday* is of two dangling objects. Perhaps the second picture is a clue as to what is being referred to here. Hebrew can be a very graphic language. The word *shaday* can also mean teats and so the overall picture is of God nourishing his children and providing all they need for life. *God of teats* has not been an acceptable image for the Bible translators, so they provide the more acceptable (though not as accurate translation) *God Almighty*.

We also see this word **el** (אל) as a suffix in a whole swathe of Old Testament names. Here are the names and their meanings:

Dani-el (God is my judge)
Jo-el (The Lord is God)
Ezeki-el (God will strengthen)
Ishma-el (God hears)
Isra-el (Struggles with God)
Immanu-el (God is with us)
Samu-el (Name of God)

Here's another one: Uzzi-el (God is my strength). He was Moses' uncle, which brings us back to our historical story.

We have talked about the two stone tablets with the Ten Words (Ten Commandments). What about the rest of God's Word? It seems that Moses wrote it himself, as instructed by God. It was an ongoing process for Moses, for the rest of his life.

He was now 120 years old. He had just handed over the mantle of leadership to young Joshua (though no spring chicken himself). He had a few more things to say, a few more things to write.

After Moses finished writing in a book the words of this law
from beginning to end, he gave this command to the Levites

who carried the ark of the covenant of the LORD: "*Take this Book of the Law and place it beside the ark of the covenant of the* LORD *your God. There it will remain as a witness against you* (Deuteronomy 31:24–26).

The book was finished – but not quite finished, of course. Joshua himself would have completed the Book of the Law with the story of the death of Moses on Mount Moab. We know that Joshua was no stranger to the writing stylus.

And Joshua recorded these things in the Book of the Law of God. Then he took a large stone and set it up there under the oak near the holy place of the LORD (Joshua 24:26).

And so was completed the written *Torah*, the "five books of Moses", from Genesis to Deuteronomy, written on scrolls and accompanying the tablets of stone in the Ark, in the Tabernacle.

This is as good a place as any to start to look at this most mis-understood of words, *Torah*. Firstly, the Hebrew letters:

תורה

Four letters, which are *tav* (t), *vav* (v), *resh* (r) and *hey* (h). The *vav* is a consonant that is sometimes a vowel (as in this case!), so you can see how the other three consonants spell out the word TRH or *Torah*, once we put in the vowels. Of course one burning question that is possibly niggling you is: who decides what vowels to put in if the Hebrew Scriptures just consist of consonants? Very good question, which will be answered ... eventually.

To say that Jews throughout history have a high view of *Torah* is akin to the statement that we need to breathe to stay alive. It is considered the holiest possession of Israel, and its place in reli-gious Jewish life is affirmed by this set prayer:

Blessed be the Lord, who has chosen us out of all the peo-ples of the world with this everlasting trust and gave us his Torah.

You'll remember what was said earlier about the three consonant root words. Well, the Hebrew word for *Torah* itself is
derived from a root verb, *yarah*:

ירה

This is made up of the letters yod (**י**), resh (**ר**) and hey (**ה**).

This is going to show us how earthy, visual and evocative
Hebrew is. This word *yarah* is basically a verb which means,
primarily, to throw or shoot, just as a skilled archer directs
his arrow on the right course. So also *Torah* is all about being
guided or directed towards the target of perfect living – it's about
instructions for life.

But aren't we taught that Torah means "law"? Yes, we are
taught this and, later, when we look at English translations of
the Bible, we'll see where this idea comes from. It's an interesting
story and worth waiting for.

This is Hebrew. It uses everyday activities and observations,
such as shooting arrows at a target, to create meaningful words
and expressions.

Hebrew verbs are interesting because Biblical Hebrew is more
about verbs than nouns. Hebrew is a dynamic language, full of
movement and expression and, as such, verbs take on a certain
level of importance. English verbs distinguish *past* (he hit me),
present (he's hitting me) and *future* (he's going to hit me). They
are all related to time. Hebrew verbs are related to *action*. Just
think how awesome this simple little fact is. Modern societies
are arranged according to our concept of time, flowing from
the past to the present to the future. We reminisce about the
past, live in the present and plan for the future. Could it be any
different? It could, but to appreciate this fully we need to think
differently – *Hebraically*. In Hebrew thought, the importance
is in the *doing* rather than "when the doing is done" (if you
can understand that). It's more important to do what you say
you're going to do, rather than abandoning it for lack of time.
Doing it late is better than not doing it at all is a very Hebraic
attitude.

Question: Why did God choose Hebrew?
Answer #3: Because it is a language of action.

Meanwhile it's back to Bible times. We've looked at some teachings, but what about the rest of the five books of Moses?

But questions, always questions. How did Moses write the rest of those five books? The "Greek-minded" would look at the *documentary hypothesis*, or at least the spirit of it. They would look at multiple authors, writing at different times and different places, with different emphases. As well as the *Yahwist* author already mentioned, they would drag in the *Elohist*, *Deuteronomist* and the *Priestly* source, all different writers, living in different places at different times. The Hebraic-minded would go along with Jesus' words, *"If you believed Moses you would believe me, for he wrote about me"* (John 5:46). But the question remains: *how* did Moses write the rest of those five books? Was it all by divine inspiration, in the sense of God dictating the words directly to him? Or did Moses have access to other sources?

Firstly, we remind ourselves where we have got to. We now know that the Ten Commandments were given by God's finger on stone tablets. What about the rest of the laws, teachings and instructions that form the bulk of Deuteronomy as well as Leviticus, Numbers and Exodus? Well we can follow the clear instructions from these very books themselves:

> *Moses then **wrote down everything** the L*ORD* had said. He got up early the next morning and built an altar at the foot of the mountain and set up twelve stone pillars representing the twelve tribes of Israel* (Exodus 24:4).

> *Then the L*ORD* said to Moses, **"Write down these words**, for in accordance with these words I have made a covenant with you and with Israel"* (Exodus 34:27).

So that accounts for much of the books of Exodus, Numbers, Leviticus and Deuteronomy, but not necessarily the historical narratives in the book of Genesis, from Creation to Joseph's multicoloured dream coat.

Of course, God could have dictated the Genesis account to Moses too, but I would be more inclined to believe that the Genesis stories were very much a part of the oral histories of the Hebrews (with the aid of clay tablets), passed down from father to son for generation after generation, starting with Adam. This has been called the "Tablet Theory".

In the 1930s, P.J. Wiseman researched the many ancient clay tablets that had been dated to the periods when the first eleven chapters in Genesis are thought to have been assembled. He found that most of these tablets had a "sign off" after every entry, naming the writer or the owner of the tablet, the subject covered, and sometimes a hint to help date the tablet. A lot of these clay tablets seemed to be dealing with family histories and Wiseman noticed how the writing style was very similar to the genealogical entries in Genesis.

These biblical genealogies are characterised by such phrases as *these are the generations of. ...* Many translators have assumed that, quite logically it seems, the description that follows is connected to the person named. This doesn't always make perfect sense in the original Hebrew and many translators have fudged things about to make sense. Wiseman had a brainwave and connected the clay tablets with these biblical records and realised that if the structure is the same then the phrase *these are the generations of* actually refers to the person named *before the phrase*! A good example is in Genesis 37:2:

> *This is the account of Jacob. Joseph, a young man of seventeen, was tending the flocks with his brothers, the sons of Bilhah and the sons of Zilpah, his father's wives, and he brought their father a bad report about them.*

It starts by saying that we are about to speak of Jacob, then it goes on to give an account of Joseph's life, *not* Jacob's life! But, instead, if Jacob's life was discussed *before* this verse, then Wiseman's theory makes sense. Which it does.

He scored on two points here as not only did this help in a tricky translation task, but it cemented these ancient biblical genealogies into real history. Suddenly, the Bible records in those early Genesis chapters could actually be speaking of *real* people!

So we can imagine Moses having a collection of these clay tablets, each created by an eye-witness to the events described, perhaps even people such as Adam, Seth and Enosh themselves. These records would have been compiled by the patriarch Jacob and brought to Egypt, where they could have been lodged in a royal archive by his son Joseph, who had risen to become a big-shot in that land. Then this would have been found by another big-shot centuries later, Moses himself. We now have ourselves a reasonable explanation of how much of those early Genesis chapters could have been compiled.

This gives many problems to those of the "Greek" mindset. Genesis chapters 1–11 have been dismissed by many as a mixture of legend, poetry and allegory. Why should this be so? From those chapters we get so much that is *foundational* to our faith, from Creation, marriage, sin and judgement to the sovereignty of God. This is important stuff and worthy of serious consideration.

The problem with the historical figures of these early chapters is that because they lived so long ago, and for what seem to be impossibly long lives, and because there is a relatively limited amount of information with which to construct well-rounded biographies, we tend to think of the accounts as legends or fables, giving room for doubts as to whether those people actually existed.

Why shouldn't they be real people? One problem with the "Greek" mind is Adam himself. It is very hard for scientists to accept the possibility of a *first man*, because their textbooks, their peers, their training and their worldview screams *evolution* and *monkeys* at them. There's no room for the flesh-and-blood Adam and a monkey-ancestor in the same mindset, despite the effort of some Christians to construct a compromise that explains micro-evolution as an acceptable tool of God in order to pander to what is widely taken to be a "scientific" view.

If you can't accept Adam as the first man, created by God, then you're going to have problems with the rest of this book.

It's all really a question of faith and submitting yourself totally, with a childlike attitude and a willingness to bypass the years of secular training that have created strata of disbelief in your mind. Otherwise that first domino will nudge the next, then the next and, before you know it, the carnage has spread into dangerous and troubling areas.

It goes something like this: Adam? *Nah, fairy tale.* Cain and Abel? *A morality tale about brothers, isn't it?* Methusaleh? *Give me a break!* Noah and the Flood? *Haven't the scientists disproved this one?* Tower of Babel? *Now you're being silly.* Abraham....

Abraham. Only one chapter after Babel ... yet isn't he the father of our faith? Didn't Jesus speak of him?

> *So those who have faith are blessed along with Abraham, the man of faith* (Galatians 3:9).

> *"I tell you the truth," Jesus answered, "before Abraham was born, I am!"* (John 8:58).

So he must have existed. Who says? If you're going to doubt Adam, Cain, Abel, Methusaleh and Noah, then why suddenly believe in Abraham? Why do we consign the first eleven chapters of Genesis to "la-la-land", yet decide that real history starts, in the next chapter, with Abraham?

Yes, Jesus speaks of Abraham. But he also speaks of Noah, Abel and Adam (by implication):

> *"As it was in the days of Noah, so it will be at the coming of the Son of Man"* (Matthew 24:37).

> *"And so upon you will come all the righteous blood that has been shed on earth, from the blood of righteous Abel to the blood of Zechariah son of Berekiah, whom you murdered between the temple and the altar"* (Matthew 23:35).

> *"Haven't you read," he replied, "that at the beginning the Creator 'made them male and female...'"* (Matthew 19:4).

We don't *pick 'n' mix* God's Word; it really is all or nothing.

Chapter Four

Lost and Found

We now consider a key question: *how do we know that the Hebrew Scriptures are 100% kosher?* How can we be totally sure that what we read is exactly *as God spoke?* This is a very pertinent question and, unfortunately, there is no definitive, testable, provable answer. Or, let me put it another way, it's the same answer to such questions as, *Is there a God?* or *Did Jesus really rise from the dead?* It's a matter of faith.

As Christians we believe in God, and who he says he is, and in Jesus, and what we're told he did. That's what defines us as Christians. The same goes for the Hebrew Scriptures. We say that we trust them, in fact, they're the tangible bedrock of our faith. But to what extent do we believe them? As the "Old Testament" in our hands is a printed translation of manuscripts originally written mainly in Hebrew, let's, first of all, focus on those manuscripts.

So we're back to Moses and his writings. He has completed (with a few additions later on by Joshua) the *Torah* – the five books of Moses – and the scrolls are kept in a safe place, with the ark of the covenant, first in the Tabernacle then in the Temple of Solomon. We read of this in Deuteronomy:

> *"Take this Book of the Law and place it beside the ark of the covenant of the LORD your God. There it will remain as a witness against you"* (Deuteronomy 31:26).

It wasn't there to gather dust, as we can see:

> *Then Moses commanded them: "At the end of every seven years, in the year for cancelling debts, during the Feast of Tabernacles, when all Israel comes to appear before the LORD your God at the place he will choose, you shall read this law before them in their hearing"* (Deuteronomy 31:10–11).

What next? Let's see what happens after the days of Moses and Joshua. Well, there's a lot of history, during which times the Hebrews fall away in things that really matter to God. They turn to those nations that surround them, people that they are warned against, even encouraged to eliminate, for good reason, it seems. They neglect the God of Abraham, Isaac and Jacob. They provoke the God of miracles to jealousy. They turn their backs on the One who guided and protected them and they demand an earthly ruler, a king. They keep the externals, the sacrificial system, but neglect the internals, a humble and contrite heart. They begin to forget the feasts of their Lord and totally forget his Words, written by human hand on scrolls in the Temple.

Around seven hundred years since the time of Moses, between the Assyrian and the Babylonian invasions, the High Priest made an incredible discovery in the Temple. Something that had been lost for a very long time was found again! Let's read:

> *Hilkiah the high priest said to Shaphan the secretary, "I have found the Book of the Law in the temple of the LORD." He gave it to Shaphan, who read it. … Then Shaphan the secretary informed the king, "Hilkiah the priest has given me a book." And Shaphan read from it in the presence of the king. When the king heard the words of the Book of the Law, he tore his robes. He gave these orders to Hilkiah the priest, Ahikam son of Shaphan, Acbor son of Micaiah, Shaphan the secretary and Asaiah the king's attendant: "Go and inquire of the LORD for me and for the people and for all Judah about what is written in this book that has been found. Great is the LORD's anger that burns against us because our fathers have not obeyed the words of this book; they have not acted in accordance with all that is written there concerning us"* (2 Kings 22:8–13).

It was the Book of the Law. Was this the five books of Moses, placed there all those centuries ago? This is a key question, because if so then we have a direct link between the author of Holy Scripture (Moses) and an incontestable historic event (King Josiah's actions leading to the discovery of the Book of the Law).

When Josiah later read out this Book of the Law *to all the people from the least to the greatest*, was he reading the very words of Moses, written around six hundred years earlier? What a thought! We have reached a crossroads, a true test of faith. Do we swing to the Hebraic way or the "Greek" path? If it is to the latter, let's get their take on this *Book of the Law* that Josiah was reading to his people.

Well, there are many theories, most appearing in the last 150 years, but few of them include Moses as an author of even a part of the books that bear his name. Not a good start. Again the *documentary hypothesis* rears its ugly head, influencing much modern scholarship. In brief, this "hypothesis" states that there are at least four sources for the content in the five books of Moses. The "J" source would have been from the 9th century BC in Judah. The "E" source would have come from the 9th century BC in Israel. Then there was the "D" source, with many potential culprits put forward, including the very same man, Hilkiah, who had discovered the Book of the Law and handed it over to King Josiah. He evidently had time to scribble his additions before the handover.

This is, of course, a massive over-simplification of all the possible ideas put forward by scholars, but none of them seeks to confirm the Word of God. I say this because there was one more source, the "P" source, put forward. This *Priestly* source is attributed to the time of the exile in Babylon, something that had not yet happened and was not going to happen *for a few decades after* the discovery of the Book of the Law.

So, if we go along with this and accept that the *Torah*, the Book of the Law, hadn't yet been put together from its four (or more) sources, what was it that Hilkiah found in the Temple? Let's not let Holy Scripture get in the way of earnest research and scholarship, shall we?

I would prefer to swing the *Hebraic* way and affirm that the Book of the Law found in the Temple was the one put there by Moses (and added to by Joshua, of course). *And why would I say that?* It is because we have a great God who is trustworthy and faithful and who would not deceive us. If God tells us that Hilkiah found *the Book of the Law* and that Moses wrote *the Book of the Law* and had it placed by the ark of the covenant, then I have perfect faith that they are *the one and the same book.* Why on earth would God want to deceive us? Why can't some people just trust what he says?

Methinks it's time for us to have another exploration of Hebrew. In the next chapter you are going to be introduced to the Hebrew alphabet, but we are going to have a sneak preview of just one of the letters: ד (*dalet*), the fourth letter. Here it is in its full glory:

ד

It started out as the following picture, in Old Canaanite:

It looks like an angular fish, but it was, in fact, a door. Here's what the picture evolved into with Old Hebrew:

From this came the Hebrew letter, ד, *dalet.* The shape of this letter is reminiscent of the upper corner of a door frame. Allied to the general meaning of "door" is the idea of a path or way of life.

It gets more interesting when we discover that *dalet* is the Hebrew word for … door.

דלת *(dalet – lamed – tav)* = **dalet** = *door, specifically the idea of hanging or swinging.*

The root verb connected to this is:

דלה *(dalet – lamed – hey)* = **dalah** = *that which hangs down, or the idea of letting down (or drawing up), as in a bucket down a well.*

From this comes the word for a bucket:

דלי *(dalet – lamed – yod)* = **daliy** = *bucket.*

This is all commonplace and mundane but the beauty of Hebrew is it can take these everyday things and take a jump. Let's look at Psalm 30:1:

I will exalt you, O LORD, for you lifted me out of the depths.

The word used for *lifted me up* is, as above:

דלה *(dalet – lamed – hey)* = **dalah**

So the mundane process of hanging down a bucket and drawing water from a well can have a spiritual application, of *being lifted up*, in the sense of being set free from despair.

The same word is used in Proverbs 20:5:

The purposes of a man's heart are deep waters, but a man of understanding draws them out.

Here we get the sense of *drawing out* the purposes of man's heart. So an everyday process known by everyone in Bible times has also been used in matters of the heart and the mind. That's the beauty of Hebrew, drawing the spiritual from the mundane.

Let's look at Psalm 141:3:

Set a guard over my mouth, O LORD; keep watch over the door of my lips.

Here the word *dalet* is used in the phrase "door of my lips", a handy and vivid description of a mouth!

Finally there's an interesting use of the word *dalet* in Jeremiah 36:23:

> *Whenever Jehudi had read three or four columns of the scroll, the king cut them off with a scribe's knife and threw them into the firepot, until the entire scroll was burned in the fire.*

The "columns" of the scroll are the leaves of a book, parchments hanging off a central spine. The word *dalet* has been used for this, for the simple reason that we have something (the "columns") hanging.

While we are on this theme let's see how Hebrew deals with emotions. Here's Psalm 6:1:

> *O* LORD, *do not rebuke me in your anger or discipline me in your wrath.*

Do you want to know what the Hebrew actually says? Of course you do:

> *O* LORD, *do not rebuke me in your **nose** or discipline me in your wrath.*

This oddity is not an oddity when you realise that Hebrew is a language of the senses. It was noticed that when one gets angry, the nostrils begin to flare and redden. So the Hebrew word for "anger" is the following:

אף *(aleph – pey)* = *aph* = nose = anger.

What other bodily parts does Hebrew make use of?

Let's start with the heart. Here's the Hebrew word:

לב *(lamed – vet)* = *lev* = heart.

The usual understanding of this is to see the heart as the *seat of emotion*. This is true, but only partly, as for the Hebrews the heart was the seat of *thought* as well as emotions. So for them, it is also performing the functions of the brain! Let's look at Deuteronomy 6:5:

> *Love the LORD your God with all your heart and with all your soul and with all your strength.*

What this is really saying is that we are not loving God just in an emotional sense, but it's a real *act of will*, with emotions and thoughts working together. This may need us to rethink a lot of Scriptures that are translated as something to do with the "heart", as it now appears that the original intention was referring to thoughts and will, not emotions!

We can get a clue to this from the original Proto-Canaanite letter pictures:

ח ۹

There's the shepherd's staff, representing "authority", and the house or home, representing "within". So we have *the authority within ourselves*, the seat of our thoughts and will, the *heart*.

Here's a strange one:

> *But, O LORD Almighty, you who judge righteously and test the heart and mind* ... (Jeremiah 11:20).

Heart and mind? Actually, in the original Hebrew it's this:

כליה *(kaph – lamed – yod – hey)* = **kilyah** = kidneys.

and

לב *(lamed – vet)* = **lev** = heart.

So the Hebrew talked about "kidneys and heart", which ends up in our Bibles as "heart and mind". Unpack that one, if you will!

For the Hebrews, the *kidneys* were seen as the main seat of emotion, whereas in our culture that's the place occupied by the heart. And, as we saw earlier, the *heart* was seen by them as the seat of thought. So, whereas the Hebrews saw the "kidneys and heart", we see the "heart and mind".

Then there are the bowels. The Hebrews saw them too as the seat of emotions, something the King James Version got right. See Jeremiah 31:20, referring to "bowels" being "troubled for him".

The NIV puts it differently, perhaps loath to use such an "unclean" word:

> ... *Therefore my heart yearns for him* ... (NIV)

So our modern English translations have expunged the earthy Hebraisms of the kidneys and bowels as being the seat of emotions and have substituted a word that conveys the same idea, but in a modern idiom. The translators have given us clarity, but they haven't translated the words as written. You can (sort of) see both sides of this one!

Question: Why did God choose Hebrew?
Answer #4: Because it is a language of the senses with simple vivid words and a direct simplicity, drawing the spiritual from the mundane.

So the year is 637 BC and the Book of the Law has been rediscovered. So what actually have they discovered? Basically, a lot of Old Hebrew writing on animal skins, but what treasures lay within!

What happened next? A complete cleansing of the kingdom. King Josiah started with the Temple and got rid of all the detestable articles and burned them. He also kicked out the pagan priests and the male prostitutes. He broke down the pagan altars, shrines and high places. He also got rid of the mediums, spiritists and household gods. Finally, he slaughtered the priests of the high places, then went back to Jerusalem and, following the instructions in the Book of the Law, celebrated Passover for the first time in centuries.

All that he did was in accordance with the instructions in the Book of the Law, the *Torah*. It was later said about Josiah that,

> *Neither before nor after Josiah was there a king like him who turned to the* LORD *as he did – with all his heart and with all his soul and with all his strength, in accordance with all the Law of Moses* (2 Kings 23:25).

This is the raw power of God's Word. There was never a king like Josiah because here was a ruler confronted by the unexpected power of the *Torah*, reading it for the first time and allowing it to embolden him, to educate him on all that had gone wrong in the kingdom before him and to empower him to put those words into action.

Perhaps we have grown jaded, perhaps we have allowed familiarity and perhaps a touch of doubt to dilute the message? We are reading the same words as Josiah did, and in many ways we are confronting the same problems that he did. Why can't we respond in the same way? He removed all pagan articles from the Temple. *Shouldn't we be doing the same with our churches and cathedrals?* He did away with the unbelieving priests. *How many of our vicars and priests are true believers in the Bible as the complete Word of God?* He desecrated the high places and pulled down the pagan altars. *What are our high places and pagan shrines now? Our celebrity culture, our sports icons, our entertainment-led society?* He pulled down the altars to Molech, the god of child-sacrifice. *Abortion and embryo research are the modern equivalent. Should we not be more concerned?*

> *For the word of God is living and active. Sharper than any double-edged sword, it penetrates even to dividing soul and spirit, joints and marrow; it judges the thoughts and attitudes of the heart* (Hebrews 4:12).

Yes, these words are alive! They speak directly to our spirit if we allow them to, if we are connected to God through covenant. Otherwise, they are just ordinary words and the Bible is just another book on the bookshelf. We must take King Josiah as an object lesson of what those words can accomplish, through a willing heart and soul.

But as good as Josiah was, it was too late to forestall the judgements that were coming to the land. The Babylonians came, destroyed the Temple and exiled the Jews. And the Book of the Law went into exile too.

We next read of the Book of the Law around seventy years later. Ezra, the priest, teacher, scribe and spiritual leader of the Jews in Babylonian exile, has been allowed back to Jerusalem by the God-fearing Persian King, Cyrus. Ezra is *well versed in the Law of Moses* (Ezra 7:6), and has *devoted himself to the study and observance of the Law of the* LORD (Ezra 7:10). You don't get to that position without access to that which you're studying, so Ezra certainly had access to the Book of the Law, as he languished in exile with his fellow Jews. Confirmation is provided in Ezra 7:14, "... *the Law of your God, which is in your hand*".

Ezra was truly a key figure. We read of him in *Legends of the Jews*, by Louis Ginzberg, Volume IV:

> *In the realisation of his second hope, the spread of the Torah, Ezra was so zealous and efficient that it was justly said of him: "If Moses had not anticipated him, Ezra would have received the Torah." In a sense he was indeed a second Moses. The Torah had fallen into neglect and oblivion in his day, and he restored and re-established it in the minds of his people.* (pp. 355f.)

Returning to Jerusalem, Ezra stood by one of the gates of the rebuilt Temple and, in front of all the people, proclaimed God's Word from the *Book of the Law of Moses*. He spoke from daybreak until noon and you can read about this in Nehemiah Chapter 8. The words had great power. Firstly, everyone wept, then, once the words had been fully explained to them, they rejoiced, feasted and celebrated the Feast of Tabernacles like never before.

Chapter Five

What Ezra did

Ezra is a key man in the story of the Hebrew Scriptures. It seems that he was the first person to really organise the compiling of God's Word into a single entity, including the writing of some Scripture himself (under the anointing of God, of course) and starting the process of replicating God's Word, as the first of the great unsung band of *Sopherim* (scribes).

Up to this point, it is fair to say that all Scripture available was 100% God's Word. All the available documents were first generation, written by whoever was inspired by God to write down his words. But from this point onward we enter a new era, an era of copying, distributing and translating God's Word by fallible human beings. However hard these scribes tried, whatever they produced was never going to be 100% accurate, maybe 99%, or even 99.99%, but *not* 100%.

One thing we can rest assured in, though, is that God's main truths will always be visible, active and uncorrupted. We can trust our God in that! It is inconceivable for those of us who believe in a faithful God to think otherwise, because to do so would render our God powerless in relation to the fallibilities and agendas of his creation.

The first thing Ezra did was change the written language. When Moses wrote the books of his name he used what we now know as *Old Hebrew*, employing an alphabet borrowed from the seafaring Phoenicians, as we saw earlier. When we get to the time of Ezra, about a thousand years later, the Jews had begun using the *Aramaic* alphabet, that being the language of exile which the Jews learned to speak in Assyria and Babylon. From this alphabet came the "square characters" of the Hebrew language, used from that time onwards in the writing of Scripture, as well as in modern forms of Hebrew.

This is as good a place as any to start looking at this alphabet. It has 22 consonants. We've already seen some of them and have even traced the origin of a few back to the pictorial forms of the ancient Canaanites. Here is a full listing of the alphabet, with their English translation, starting with the first six. (For reference, the whole alphabet is on show in the Appendix, at the end of this book).

א aleph

This has no sound of its own, despite seemingly being the equivalent to the English vowel, "a". Remember, these are all consonants – we will be discussing vowels later on (though, just to confuse you, the aleph had also been used as a part-time vowel before vowels were invented!) As we saw earlier, this letter mutated from the Canaanite picture of an ox head, signifying leadership and strength. It is also used for counting, with the numerical value of 1.

ב bet/vet

This has two possible sounds. If it has a dot (called a *dagesh*) in the middle then it is a "b" sound (*bet*), otherwise it is a "v" sound (*vet*). So a ב is a "b" and a ב is a "v". This one mutated from a picture of a tent or a house. It has the numerical equivalent of 2.

ג gimmel

This third letter is a "g", not the expected "c", a hard sound as in "girl". This letter came from the picture of a camel (similar name), though it can also be a foot. It has the number value of 3.

ד dalet

As might be expected, this is a "d" sound, as in "door", which is the picture that it came from. It was originally seen as a door hanging down from a frame. It has the number value of 4.

ה **hey**

This was originally depicted as a man with outstretched arms, perhaps calling out "hey!" (though maybe not, as they didn't speak English!) This is an "h" sound, called a *guttural* letter as it is formed from the back of the throat. All languages have their eccentricities and a *hey* at the end of a word is normally a silent letter. Also, as with the *aleph*, the *hey* sometimes functions as a part-time vowel letter. It also has the number value of 5.

ו **vav**

Here is a letter that actually does resemble its original word picture, that of a tent peg, or nail. It has the sound of a "v" and represents the number 6.

Here's a fun legend on how the aleph got to be the first letter of the Hebrew alphabet.

God decided it was time to put the letters in some sort of order, so he asked each one in turn why it should be the first.

"*I'm tallest,*" cried the lamed, "*and the others will be able to see my waving crown all down the line.*"

"*No,*" said the shin, "*I should be first because I have three crowns and the people should behold my glory first.*"

And on it went down the line (or, rather, no line because they weren't in order yet!)

After all the letters had given their case for being the first, God noticed that the bet hadn't spoken.

"*So what's your reason?*" God inquired.

"*Oh, Lord, I have no reason. I can think of no way that I'm so special I should go first.*"

"*Then you will,*" said God. "*My chosen ones will be a humble people and you are a humble letter.*"

Then he noticed one of them was missing. "*Aleph, where are you?*" They finally found the aleph in one corner of the heavens.

"*Where were you? Didn't I call all the letters together?*"

"*Oh Lord, I can't even make a sound. I don't even deserve to be in the company of the other letters, and I barely even have a crown.*"

God was so pleased by this display of humility that he placed *aleph*, the silent letter, at the head of the parade of letters, with *bet* following close behind. And that's how we got the Hebrew *aleph-bet* (alphabet)!

Back to the "aleph-bet" now. Here are the next five of them.

ז zayin
This is the letter "z" and mutated from a picture of a weapon, which it still largely resembles. This is not to be confused with a *vav* drawn with a shaky hand! It has the number value of 7.

ח chet
The first unusual letter sound. This is a "ch" as in Bach, another guttural letter from the back of the throat, with a light scraping sound. It was originally the picture of a fence or an inside room of a house. It has the number value of 8.

ט tet
This was originally a twisting snake, something you can just about imagine. It also meant "to surround". It is a "t" sound and represents the number 9.

י yod
This name rhymes with "rod" and is the letter "y". It was originally seen as a hand and was associated with works or deeds. It's another of those letters that sometimes functioned as a vowel in the early days. It has the number equivalent of 10.

כ kaph/khaph
As with the *bet*, this is another one with two possible sounds. If it has the dot (dagesh) in the middle, כּ, it is a *kaph* and is pronounced "k". Without the dagesh, כ, it is a *khaph* and is pronounced close enough to the "ch" as in the *chet*. This letter also has an added eccentricity in that it looks different at the end of a word. This is called a *sofit* form and it looks like this: ך. It was originally seen as the palm of a hand or a wing, or in the action "to open" and has the number value of 20 (not 11, although it's

the eleventh letter) and, to add even more to the confusion, the *sofit* form has the number value of 500!

OK, we're halfway there now. This is all just for reference, I don't expect you to remember all of this – there is no exam. All that you need at this stage is an appreciation of the building blocks of the language.

As a point of interest, there is a mystical tradition in *kabbalah* that the twenty-two Hebrew letters are so sacred and powerful that they were the main building blocks that God used in the Creation of the world. It's all down to letters, words and phrases combined in certain ways. Even Adam's naming of the animals had significance in this way. Of course, this is mystical tradition and not biblical revelation, so it's useful only to remind us of how seriously the sages took their language and traditions. It is a dangerous area to explore – to be avoided at all costs.

Now for the second half. ...

ל lamed
Here's the shepherd's staff or cattle goad and it represents the idea of control or guidance. It is the "l" sound, as in "look" and has the number equivalent of 30.

מ mem
If you concentrate on the top of this letter and draw it out to the left and right you could imagine the undulations of the waves on the sea, which is where this letter comes from. It is a picture of water. It's another letter with a different look (*sofit*) at the end of a word, where it takes the form ם. It is the "m" sound and represents the number 40, with the *sofit* form representing 600.

נ nun
This is pronounced "noon" and is the "n" sound. It's another one with a *sofit* form at the end of a word: ן. This was originally a fish and you really do need to stretch your imagination this time. It helps if the fish is seen to be swimming vertically. It also signifies activity or life. It represents the number 50, with the *sofit* form representing 700.

ס samech

This is a tricky design, being very similar to the *sofit* form of the *mem*, so it must be a bit of a nightmare for scribes, particularly when at the end of a word. It signifies a prop or support, again difficult to imagine. It is the letter "s" and is also the number 60.

ע ayin

An interesting name as, indeed, it originally had the meaning of an "eye", though the visual transformation had been quite an extreme one. It also had the meaning of seeing or understanding. Like the *aleph* it's a silent letter, seen but not heard. It represents the number 70.

פ pey/phey

Another double letter. With the dagesh, **פ**, it is a "p" sound (*pey*) and without it, **פ**, it becomes a "ph" sound (*phey*). It's another letter with a *sofit* form, ף. It represents a mouth and the act of speaking. It is the number 80 and the *sofit* form has the value of 800.

צ tsade

This is a fishhook or, interestingly, a man on his side. It is pronounced as "ts" (as in "nuts") and has a *sofit* form of ץ. It is the number 90 and the *sofit* form is 900.

ק qoph

This is a similar sound to the כ (*kaph*) but is usually represented by a "q", as in "queen" and is derived from a picture of the back of a man's head, or, alternatively, the sun on the horizon. It is the number 100.

ר resh

This is the "r" sound and depicts a man's head (the front, not the back) and represents the idea of importance or priority. It is the number 200.

ש shin/sin

This one depicts teeth (you can see that) and conveys the sense of eating or consuming (or destroying). It's another double letter but different from the others with regard to the positioning of the dot. If the dot is in the upper-right position, ‎שׁ, it's a "sh" sound (*shin*), if it's in the upper-left position, it's a ‎שׂ, a "s" sound (*sin*). Both have a numerical value of 300.

‎ת tav

Finally we have the "t" sound, meaning a sign or a mark. It is the number 400.

Returning to the alphabet list, to our Greek logical minds there's a lot of implied vagueness here. For a start there's not total agreement as to what some of the letters originally represented, as – let's face it – we're talking about the birth of writing here so there are not likely to have been many academics and scholars around back then whom we can research! We can also see some letters with two possible sounds and some sounds with two possible letters. *What's all this about, can't it all be nice and logical like English* (the language that gives us the little word 'bar' with apparently 36 different meanings!)?

This book is not intended as a Hebrew primer. I intend to give you just enough knowledge to whet your appetite without drowning you, and enough to appreciate the beauty and strengths of Hebrew. Now every language has its quirks and idiosyncrasies – we have already met the main ones, the *dagesh* and the *sofit* and the double letters – and, if you are curious, dive into a book of Hebrew grammar if you want bedside reading guaranteed to send you off into slumber-land! Then there's the matter of the vowels. You'll have to be patient with me on this one.

What did the "Greek" mind think of Ezra, the man chiefly responsible for the use of this alphabet in the Hebrew Scriptures? Well, the documentary hypothesis concedes his existence, which is a good start. It also identifies him as possibly one of the writers of the Hebrew Scriptures, the "P" (Priestly) source. So at least there's one point where biblical evidence ties in with academic scholarship!

So Ezra rewrote the Book of the Law in the new Hebrew alphabet of "square characters", as well as the Books of *Ezra* and *Chronicles*. But he was not a man alone. He seems to be one of the prime movers in an institution that has become known as *The Great Synagogue* or *The Great Assembly*. There's a lot of haziness about who they were (there were said to be 120 of them at any given time – the same number as the current Israeli parliament, the *Knesset*) or how long they lasted, but it seems there is more agreement as to what their achievements were. Here are a few of them:

- Created many of the benedictions and prayers of the Jewish liturgy.
- Established the festival of Purim (the story in the Book of Esther).
- Achieved the beginning of the creation of a canon for the "Old Testament" (i.e. deciding which books to include). Included, apart from the *Torah*, the Books of Ezekiel, Daniel, Esther and the Twelve minor prophets.

In the *Talmud* (*Baba Bathra* 14, 15a) a list was given as to the identity of the authors of the other books of the Hebrew Scriptures. Make what you like of their viewpoint.

> *Who wrote the Holy Books? Moses wrote his book, the section concerning Bileam and Job. Jehoshua wrote his book and eight verses in the Law. Samuel wrote his book, the book of Judges and Ruth. David wrote the book of Psalms by means of ten Ancients, Adam, the first, Melchisedech, Abraham, Moses, Heman, Iduthun, Asaph and the three sons of Kore. Jeremias wrote his books, the Book of Kings and the Lamentations. Ezechias and his colleagues wrote Isaias, Proverbs, the Canticles of Canticles, and Ecclesiastes. The men of the Great Synagogue wrote Ezekiel, the twelve Prophets, Daniel, and the volume of Esther. Ezra wrote his book, and continued the genealogies of the Chronicles up to his time.*

It is not worth going into detail as to authors, as the above is just speculation. We should trust that God ensured that his words were written down, and that Ezra and the scribes who followed him were diligent in their work in ensuring that the words were the correct ones.

The most curious of the pronouncements of the Great Assembly was the holding of twenty-four fasts to pray that the *Sopherim* (scribes) should not become too rich to ignore their duties of copying Holy Scripture!

It's worth mentioning a group who split away from the mainstream Jewish community, as a result of the population movements caused by the exiles into Assyria and Babylonia. These were the *Samaritans* – and they weren't all good! Some were probably downright awful and all of them were very much outsiders. They were a mixed race, claiming ancestry from the Israelites, and they lived in the central part of Israel, the area called *Samaria* at the time of Jesus. They had two distinctions. Firstly, they worshipped not in Jerusalem but at Mount Gerizim, near Shechem, and secondly, in line with their name that translates as "Keepers of (the Law)", they recognised *just* the *Torah*, the "Law", the five books of Moses, and nothing else.

In 1616 AD, a manuscript was discovered in Damascus. It became known as the *Samaritan Pentateuch* (or the Samaritan *Torah*) and was a complete copy of the *Torah* but written using the Samaritan variation of the Hebrew alphabet. It is the oldest complete copy of the *Torah*, but there's a problem in that there are around 6,000 differences to the *Masoretic* text (the most accepted version – more on this later) of the Hebrew Scriptures. Some of these differences have been useful for scholars on certain tricky passages, so it is not without some value in the great scheme of things. A reason why scholars can't take this manuscript too seriously is that it is thought that some of the variations could be deliberate on theological or cultural grounds. This is particularly obvious in an added Scripture, just after Exodus 20:17, a commandment to *build a sanctuary on Mount Gerizim*!

But that is just a distraction. We are more interested in the story of Holy Scripture. So, in the next Chapter, we are going to explore the process initiated by Ezra and his *Sopherim*, and see where that takes us.

Chapter Six
The First Scribes

If you're a fan of police procedural TV shows, such as CSI, you'll be familiar with the term *the chain of custody*. It's a paper trail, following a piece of evidence at every stage of its journey, without any gaps. This is what we've been doing with God's Word, using evidence supplied by the very words themselves. In a way the *chain of custody* ended with Ezra, as from this point forwards the *Sopherim* start to create new copies of the original source document and we have no way of knowing where each individual copy ended up.

What about these *Sopherim*? The original meaning of this word was "people who know how to write" but the rabbis also took a meaning from the word *sophar*, to count. This is interesting and highly descriptive because a *Sopher* really needed to know how to count. When copying God's Word onto a new scroll they needed to count every single Hebrew letter in many different ways to ensure that they had made no mistakes. It appears that there was a lot at stake. A certain Rabbi Ishmael was said to have told a *Sopher*, "*My son, be careful in thy work, as it is a heavenly work, lest thou err in omitting or adding one iota, and so cause the destruction of the whole world*" (Er. 13a).

A strange thing to say, methinks, as an iota is the ninth letter in the *Greek* alphabet. Why should a Rabbi refer to Greek? (Thought I'd ask, though I don't expect an answer.) But it does bring to mind a very famous saying of Jesus, which is worth looking at here:

> *"I tell you the truth, until heaven and earth disappear, not
> the smallest letter, not the least stroke of a pen, will by any
> means disappear from the Law until everything is accom-
> plished"* (Matthew 5:18 NIV).

The King James Version is more specific, speaking of one "jot"
or one "tittle" here. This word *jot* is actually referring to the
iota, the smallest Greek letter. But this saying of Jesus was not
originally in Greek, it was most likely in Hebrew, or he at least
was making a reference to the Hebrew alphabet. He was actually
referring to the smallest Hebrew letter, the *yod*.

׳

The word *tittle* translates from the Greek word *keraia*, meaning
"horn", which refers to the smallest stroke of a Hebrew letter, a
tiny squiggle or flourish that the *Sopher* made when finishing a letter, such as the embellishment at the top left-hand edge of a ב, ד or
כ or the subtle difference between the נ (nun) and ג (gimmel).

The early *Sopherim* were also on a holy mission, in their eyes.
They wanted to ensure that there would be no more exiles from
the Land and so had to make sure that there could be no more
forsaking of the *Torah*, all 613 commandments of it. So they
built a hedge or fence around these commandments, in the form
of more instructions and laws and regulations. This became the
oral law, or the Traditions of the Elders, eventually written down
as the *Mishnah* and other writings.

The *Sopher* had to be at the top of his game when copying
text. He had to work from an original template document and
was not allowed in any sense to rely on his memory. *Let thine
eyes look right on, and let thine eyelids look straight before thee*
(Proverbs 4:25) is the advice once given by a rabbi to a *Sopher*
whom he saw writing a scroll from memory. He added, *Indeed
thou art able to write the whole Torah by heart; but our sages
have forbidden the writing of even one letter without an exem-
plar* (Meg. 18b).

These exacting standards have been maintained ever since,
with the *Sopherim* of today still working under these same con-

ditions. And because of the efforts of these early *Sopherim*, we can be confident that subsequent generations of God's Word, copied onto scrolls or parchment from a master template kept in the Temple, are going to be as accurate as is humanly possible, so that the very words of Moses can be read as close as possible to those written many hundreds of years earlier.

There remains today an example of their work. It is called the Nash papyrus, a collection of four fragments found in Egypt at the end of the 19th Century, by the secretary of the Society of Biblical Archaeology, a certain W. L. Nash. This was certainly the oldest manuscript fragment found, dating back to around 150 BC, until the Dead Sea Scrolls came along (more on those later).

It contained the Hebrew text of the Ten Commandments, as well as some more Scripture from the books of Exodus and Deuteronomy, specifically the *Shema*, one of the most important Scriptures (even now) for Jewish people.

Let's have a little look at the Shema. It's from Deuteronomy 6:4 and it is the main prayer in the *Siddur*, the Jewish prayer book. It's considered so holy that it's the prayer on the lips of many a Jewish martyr and, when recited in the synagogue, Orthodox Jews cover their eyes with their right hand. The core part of it is here, just six words:

שמע	ישראל	יהוה	אלהינו	יהוה	אחד
shema	Yisrael	Adonai	Eloheynu	Adonai	echad
Hear!	O Israel	the Lord	our God	the Lord	is one

Now for the *"English"* way round (i.e. left to right): **Hear O Israel, the Lord, Our God, the Lord, is One.**

There's a lot one could say about this simple prayer; much has been written about it in both Jewish and Christian circles.

שמע ישראל יהוה אלהינו יהוה אחד

On *Torah* scrolls today, two Hebrew letters stand out, the *ayin* (ע) in "shema" and the *dalet* (ד) in "echad". They are enlarged as they spell out another Hebrew word:

עֵד

This visible reminder, *ed*, takes the meaning of "witness", high-lighting the need for this prayer to be a witness or a testimony to our God.

As for the words to the *shema* themselves, let's consider them in turn. The first is the word from which the prayer is named:

שְׁמַע *(shin – mem – ayin)* = **shema** = *hear*.

This word is far more powerful than it seems. It's not a case of just *hearing* but the actions that proceed from that process. It is about *obeying* God, in fact that is another meaning for *shema* elsewhere in Scripture. Hebraic understanding has no truck with *just* hearing but what effects the Word of God has on you. If you are not moved to action, then you haven't *really* heard.

יִשְׂרָאֵל *(yod – sin – resh – aleph – lamed)* = **Yisrael** = *O Israel*.

We have seen the suffix, *el* (אֵל), before. It's the word for "God". So what about the beginning of the word? Actually it's not that straightforward. In fact it seems that we are dealing with quite a special word here, which is fitting, I suppose, as it is dealing with a fairly special people. The first half of the word is based on the following:

שָׂרָה *(sin – resh – hey)* = **sara**.

The meaning of this word has to be taken from the context in which it is used here. After all, it is a very strange context when one looks at how this name came to be. It's taken from Genesis 32:28, the patriarch Jacob's wrestling match with God at Peniel.

> *Then the man said, "Your name will no longer be Jacob, but Israel, because you have struggled with God and with men and have overcome."*

The word *Israel* seems from the context to mean "struggles with God", implying that the Hebrew word *sara* takes the meaning of "struggling". The actual root of this word, *sar*, can take the meaning of "prevailing" or "persisting" (as well as "prince"). An alternative meaning has been suggested – that it is actually God who has persisted (with Jacob) rather than Jacob struggling with God. Hey, this is Hebrew, it's not meant to be all cut and dried! We just have to understand that the name *Israel* has been born out of conflict between man and God and implies that any further dealings between these two protagonists is going to be, to say the least, interesting. And biblical history (and subsequent world history) has certainly borne this out!

יהוה *(yod – hey – vav– hey)* = ?

This word appears twice. It is a very important word. It is God's personal name and there's more to say about this a bit later on.

אלהינו *(aleph – lamed – hey – yod – nun–vav)* = *eloheynu* = our God(s).

Again we have already seen this word, in a slightly different form, at the end of the first phrase in the Ten Commandments. It was:

אלהיך

It translates as "Your God" and again we can see the *elohim* (אלהים) part, the *plural* word that is used to refer to God in Genesis 1:1 and allows us to think a lot about the Trinity.

Our final word has been a great talking point and it is the most talked about word in the *shema* by Christians.

אחד *(aleph – chet – dalet)* = *echad* = one, alone.

Here there might seem to be a problem. If *echad* means "one", then there is just one God. So how does that fit in with the biblically revealed truth of the Holy Trinity? There is in reality no problem here because Christians do believe that God is One, in the sense that we, like the Hebrews, are monotheistic. But it is also true and must be said that Christians know and encounter God as three persons in one God. We know him as God the Father, as Jesus [*Yeshua*] the Son of God and as Holy Spirit of God, and Christian believers find that to be true in their own spiritual experience and in God's Word too – and we find that great truth throughout the "Old Testament" as well as the "New".

We have covered the Nash papyrus and hopefully you now have a better understanding of the *Shema*. What else do we know about those early *Sopherim*, who operated in that period of time that straddled the "Old" and "New" Testaments? Not a lot, apparently. It would have been interesting, though, to know what they thought about the first serious attempt at translating their precious Scriptures into an alien language, namely Greek. This is where we go to next.

Chapter Seven

Going Global

Most Jews didn't return with Ezra and the others to the promised land but stayed in exile, in Babylon and other places. Within a century or so they were quite cosy in their new environments. Many even stopped speaking Hebrew. In particular, those living in Alexandria in Egypt were so influenced by the Greek culture that surrounded them that they became pretty good Greek speakers. The rabbis were horrified, the identity of their people was being dissolved and assimilated. They were even losing interest and knowledge of their Holy Scriptures. Something had to be done about this.

There are two versions of what happened next, the real version and the fanciful version. The latter gave its name to a very famous translation of the Hebrew Scriptures and, for this reason, is the commonly accepted scenario. The name is *Septuagint*, from the Latin word for "seventy" and is usually known simply by the Roman numerals for this number: *LXX*.

The name derives from a persistent legend, told in the *Letter of Aristeas*, which is summarised thus (in the *Talmud, Tractate Megillah 9*):

> *King Ptolemy once gathered 72 Elders. He placed them in 72 chambers, each of them in a separate one, without revealing to them why they were summoned. He entered each one's room and said: "Write for me the Torah of Moshe (Moses), your teacher." God put it in the heart of each one to translate identically as all the others did.*

So, allegedly, the Greek ruler, Ptolemy II, contacted the High

Priest in Jerusalem and asked for 72 Jewish translators (six from each tribe) to translate the Books of Moses from Hebrew to Greek. He took them to an isolated island, separated them for 72 days and told them to get on with it. The result was "beautiful, devout and accurate" and a worthy addition to the great library at Alexandria. That was the legend and the origin of the name, though it seems they were as inaccurate in their naming of this book (the name is derived from the number 70, not 72!) as the apparent quality of the translation.

The real origin is the obvious one mentioned earlier, *not* the legend from the *Talmud*. The Jews in the Greek-speaking world needed a translation of their own Scriptures in a language they actually used! The *Torah* was translated first, followed over a longer period by the Prophetic books and the Writings. It wasn't the best translation ever but was hugely influential, particularly as it was quoted in the Gospels (though not extensively). This may not have qualified it as *100% God-inspired*, but certainly the parts quoted in the New Testament must have been, otherwise God wouldn't have allowed them to be used.

Experts generally agree that the Septuagint was written by a varied group of translators, as there is a real lack of uniformity in how the individual books were translated. These people show a variety of styles, translation methods, even proficiency in Hebrew. Some books are translated better than others and some have glaring errors.

For example, the Book of Jeremiah lacks around 2,700 words that are in the original Hebrew and some verses appear in a different order to other later translations from the Hebrew. Also Job is said to have huge gaps in it and Daniel and Isaiah are not served too well either. A factor in all of these problems is that the Hebrew documents used as source material weren't the most accurate available. But at that time it was an influential piece of work. In fact it was the *first translation* of any sacred book into another language and said to be one of the most significant events in religious history, despite many later commentators casting doubts on the quality of the source material the translators had to work from. There will be more on these points later.

Not only could many Jews now rediscover their heritage, but the Hebrew Scriptures were also opened up to Gentiles in the Greek-speaking world. Did you really believe that the Ethiopian eunuch was a Hebrew reader? Very unlikely, it was surely the Septuagint he was reading from, as a eunuch would not be allowed into the Jewish community (Deuteronomy 23:1).

> *Now an angel of the Lord said to Philip, "Go south to the road – the desert road – that goes down from Jerusalem to Gaza." So he started out, and on his way he met an Ethiopian eunuch, an important official in charge of all the treasury of Candace, queen of the Ethiopians. This man had gone to Jerusalem to worship, and on his way home was sitting in his chariot reading the book of Isaiah the prophet* (Acts 8:26–28).

The Septuagint became the "official" Old Testament for the early church, a somewhat ironic state of affairs for Jews at that time as Christian apologists used this translation in many disputes with them, particularly in reference to contentious verses, such as Isaiah 7:14 ("virgin" or "young woman"?), that were interpreted differently in their own Hebrew Scriptures. The Christians would look at them in such disputes and say: *Hey, it was your people who gave us the Septuagint so why are you arguing against it?*

Also, in the New Testament, when the "Old Testament" is being quoted from, it is usually from the Septuagint. So, whatever shortcomings it may have, the Holy Spirit was pleased to use it at key points in the New Testament narrative. God will always work with the work of our hands, despite our frailties and defects! Thank goodness for that!

But let's ask a very pertinent question about the Septuagint that has rarely been asked. *Can the Hebraic thoughts in the Hebrew Scriptures be adequately expressed in another language, namely Greek in this case?* It's a very relevant question because the Hebrew and Greek mindsets are not exactly welcome bedfellows. The translators did their best, and only the hindsight of future reflection can decide whether their best was good enough. This is surely going to be a recurrent theme every time the Hebrew Scriptures are translated into another language, whatever it is ... *even English*, "God's own language" (according to the English!)

There were places where there simply weren't Greek words available. Some Hebrew words, such as *cherubim* or *shabbat* were simply transliterated. In other cases, Greek words were even invented, such as a word for foreskin! Some passages were wonderfully translated, others became a bit of a "dog's dinner"! Some Hebrew idioms and sayings were totally lost in translation, and in other places Greek understanding clouded the original Hebrew context. An example of this is in Genesis 23:11, the sale of the Cave of Machpelah:

> *"No, my lord," he said. "Listen to me; I give you the field, and I give you the cave that is in it. I give it to you in the presence of my people. Bury your dead."*

In the Septuagint, *"in the presence of my people"* became *"before all my fellow citizens"*. The idea of a "citizen" is a totally Greek political concept and hardly something relevant to desert nomads in the age of the Patriarchs!

No original manuscripts of the Septuagint have survived history. The early church loved it and, consequently, the Jews hated it. They were holding out for something better.

Meanwhile, back to the Land of Israel. It was AD 70 and Rabbi Johanan ben Zakkai was one of the most important Jewish sages of his day, important enough to be smuggled out of a Jerusalem currently being besieged and soon to be destroyed by the Roman army. Through shrewd manoeuvring he managed to secure a safe haven for himself and his fellow sages at Yavneh (also called Jamnia), on the Mediterranean coast. It was at Yavneh that Judaism survived the onslaught of the Romans. Ben Zakkai and others created a form of Judaism, *Rabbinic Judaism*, that could survive the loss of the Jerusalem Temple and the animal sacrifices, replacing them with prayer, encouraged by Hosea 6:6:

> *For I desire mercy, not sacrifice, and acknowledgment of God rather than burnt offerings.*

Out of this came a great revival in that small town, resulting in a council held at around 90 AD, when the *canon* of the Hebrew Scriptures was set. Much debate was had over four of the intended books that were considered "marginal". These were Proverbs, Ecclesiastes, Esther and the Song of Solomon. But, in actual fact, the deliberations of that Council were not as crucial as may seem as most of the books that finally made it into the Canon had already been deemed God-inspired and authoritative for some time.

The Hebrew Bible was divided into three sections. First, the *Torah*:

תורה *(tav – vav – resh – hey)* = **torah** = *teaching.*

This comprises the five books of Moses: *Genesis* (Bereshit), *Exodus* (Shemot), *Leviticus* (Vayikra), *Numbers* (Bemidbar) and *Deuteronomy* (Devarim).

In each case, the Hebrew name has been given in brackets. Each name is, in fact, the first main Hebrew word in the book. The names that we know them as (Genesis, Exodus, etc.) are the ones given in the Septuagint, based on the theme of each book.

So the first book is known as "In the Beginning" in the Hebrew Bible, but *Genesis* in the Christian "Old Testament", meaning "Origin". The second book is known as "Names" to the Jews, but *Exodus* to the Christians, meaning "going out". The third book is known as "And he called" to the Jews, but *Leviticus* to the Christians, meaning "relating to the Levites". The fourth book is known as "In the desert" to the Jews, but *Numbers* to the Christians. Finally, the last book is known as "These are the words" to the Jews, but *Deuteronomy* to the Christians, meaning "second law".

The second section is *Nevi'im*:

נביאים *(nun – vet –yod – aleph – yod – mem)* = *nevi'im* = *prophets.*

First there are the usual suspects: *Isaiah, Jeremiah* and *Ezekiel*. Then also included are some of the historical books: *Joshua, Judges, Samuel* (I and II combined) and *Kings* (I and II combined). Then there are the rest of the prophets, all combined together in one sub-section called "The Twelve Prophets". These are the books of *Hosea, Joel, Amos, Obadiah, Jonah, Micah, Nahum, Habakkuk, Zephaniah, Haggai, Zechariah* and *Malachi*. There is one notable omission: *Daniel* is not considered a book of prophecy. As Christians we should find this intriguing and suspicious because *doesn't Daniel 9:25 give a pretty good estimate as to when the Jewish Messiah would appear?* (For more of that, I refer you to my book, *Jesus, Man of Many Names*). Is that not prophecy, uncomfortable as it is?

The third section is *Ketuvim*:

כתובים *(kaph – tav – vav – vet – yod– mem)* = *ketuvim* = *writings.*

These are, in turn, divided into three sub-groups. The *Wisdom* comprises the books of *Psalms, Proverbs* and *Job*, also known as the poetic books. The *Megillot* are the five scrolls, the books of *Song of Songs, Ruth, Lamentations, Ecclesiastes* and *Esther*, and they have a special place in the Jewish liturgical year. The Song of Songs is read out at Passover time, Ruth at Shavuot (Pentecost), Lamentations at Tisha B'Av, Ecclesiastes at Sukkot (Tabernacles) and Esther at Purim. Finally, last but not least are *Daniel, Ezra-Nehemiah* (combined into one book) and *Chronicles* (I and II).

When we take these three section names together, we get the Hebrew name for the whole thing:

Torah
Nevi'im
Ketuvim

These create the acronym *Tanak* (or *Tenach*), the Hebrew name for the *Hebrew Scriptures*.

The Books in the *Tenach* are exactly the same content as in our Christian "Old Testament" but in a different order. Jesus himself alluded to the Jewish book order in the following:

> *"Therefore this generation will be held responsible for the blood of all the prophets that has been shed since the beginning of the world, from the blood of Abel to the blood of Zechariah, who was killed between the altar and the sanctuary"* (Luke 11:50–51).

Here Jesus speaks of *Abel* (from the first book, Bereshit – Genesis) to *Zechariah* (from the last book, Chronicles), to give the impression of the whole sweep of the Hebrew Scriptures. The three-fold division of the *Tenach* is also implied in Jesus' remark to his disciples:

> *He said to them, "This is what I told you while I was still with you: Everything must be fulfilled that is written about me in the Law of Moses, the Prophets and the Psalms"* (Luke 24:44).

So the Council at Yavneh rubber-stamped the completed Canon of the Hebrew Scriptures, the *Tenach*. Let's take ourselves back to that time and look through the eyes of a learned Jew. What would he see? The main difference between the Hebrew letters and words, as fixed by this Council, and the ones that we would see now if we were to open up a current "Old Testament" written in Hebrew is that there were *no vowels at that time, just consonants* (although three of them ה, ו and י served as vowels in a limited sense).

How on earth did they manage to pronounce the words without vowels? Good question, but with an obvious answer. They had a very exhaustive oral tradition at that time; Scripture was memorised from a very early age. In short, most knew the Scriptures by heart, so vowels weren't needed. This seems as good an answer as any and held water at least for a few centuries. But then there's the *Chinese whispers* syndrome – if you rely solely on oral traditions, pronunciation of some words could change, particularly as Jews were moving around a lot and being exposed to a whole gamut of strange tongues.

And there was one word that was *not* to be pronounced. Ever! This was the very name of God Himself. Here it is. Read it and tremble:

יהוה Yod – Hey – Vav – Hey

This name appears 6,828 times in the Hebrew Scriptures. Who says that the Scriptures are not God-breathed? He is all over them! The name first appears in Genesis 2:4:

> *This is the account of the heavens and the earth when they were created. When the* LORD *God made the earth and the heavens.*

Whenever we see the word LORD (written in small capitals), the Hebrew word is יהוה, God's name.

Here is where God spells out the deal, explaining himself and who he is, in his encounter with Moses at the burning bush.

> *Moses said to God, "Suppose I go to the Israelites and say to them, 'The God of your fathers has sent me to you,' and they ask me, 'What is his name?' Then what shall I tell them?" God said to Moses, "I AM WHO I AM. This is what you are to say to the Israelites: 'I AM has sent me to you'"* (Exodus 3:13–14).

Interestingly and contrary to popular belief, the Hebrew word used in this passage, where God mentions his name, is not יהוה. So, what's going on here? Is it his name or isn't it? In this Exodus passage, the word used for his name is this:

אהיה Aleph – Hey – Yod – Hey

This takes the meaning of "I will be" (although the English translations are usually "I am"). I have no intention of delving into metaphysical areas, so let's just be content in the understanding that God is just ... *God* and doesn't need any further explanation. This word shares a similar three-consonant root with יהוה (Hey – Vav – Hey and Hey – Yod – Hey), which should be enough to convince our uneducated minds (well, *mine* anyway) that they are related and both are ways of describing Almighty God.

So יהוה is the sacred name of God. In Bible times it was only ever uttered during worship in the Jerusalem Temple, particularly on the Day of Atonement, when the High Priest pronounced it ten times, according to the *Talmud* (*Tosef.*, *Yoma* ii. 2, *Yoma* 39b). So at that time the pronunciation of the sacred name was known, particularly as the *Talmud* has many warnings about uttering the name. It was also considered to have special powers of healing.

Finally, we will remember that the sacred name is the middle word in that first statement by him in the Ten Commandments:

אנכי יהוה אלהיך"*I am the* LORD *your God*"

You'll notice that the English translation substitutes the word LORD for the sacred name. Later on we are going to see how many Christians were not happy with this and endeavoured to figure out the exact pronunciation of God's name. But did they get it right? We will find out more in Chapter Nine.

Let's think about the use of numbers. Earlier, when we covered the Hebrew alphabet, we saw how every letter represented a number. The first nine letters represented the numbers 1 to 9, then the next few were multiples of ten, i.e. 20, 30, 40 etc. Then there are multiples of 100. To see how this operates, if you want to represent the number 19, you add a *yod* (number 10) to a *tet* (number 9). That's all very well, but, in the case of the numbers 15 and 16, something very different happens.

The logical way of producing a 15 is to add a *yod* (number 10) to a *hey* (number 5), and similarly with a 16 (adding a *yod* to a *vav*) but this never happens. Why? Because these letters are part of the sacred name and there would be every possibility of accidentally writing this name. So, instead, a 15 is made up of a *tav* (9) and a *vav* (6) and a 16 is made up of a *tav* (9) and a *zayin* (7). Can you imagine any other people in the history of the world who would create a numbering system that was reverent to their deity?

One final word concerning the *Sopher* and his dedication to his work and his God. Before writing the sacred name he must first pause for prayer and reflection and then must write the name down without interruption. If he makes a mistake, he must not correct it as he would any other word but the whole page must be discarded and buried in a *genizah* (burial place for damaged and old scrolls). Then the page is restarted.

But there was a *new kid on the block*, the Gentile church. These Christians also had their eye on the Hebrew Scriptures. They couldn't read Hebrew (apart from the Jewish Christians in the early years) and so were grateful for the Greek translation, the *Septuagint*. But not all of them. Some were openly critical, because, as we have already seen, the Hebrew sources used were not as accurate as those that became the Canon at the Council of Yavneh. One church Father, *Origen*, though, was helpful enough to create perhaps the world's first comparative Bible, so that people could check it out for themselves.

This was the *Hexapla*, which had six varieties of the "Old Testament" side by side. First, there were the Hebrew Scriptures, then the same but transliterated into Greek, then the Greek translation of *Aquila*, followed by the Greek translation of *Symmachus*, then the Septuagint, then the Greek translation of *Theodotion*. Sadly, as with the Septuagint, no copies of this have survived to the present day and the original was probably destroyed when the Muslims invaded Caesarea in 638 AD.

So, who were these new people who had taken on responsibility for translating the Hebrew Scriptures into Greek? Aquila was a Gentile Christian who converted to Judaism at around 130 AD, becoming a follower of Rabbi Akiva. As a result, his very literal translation was more popular among the Jews than the Christians and he showed where his loyalties lay in his translating of a *key word* in Isaiah 7:14 as "young woman" rather than "virgin" (more of this controversy later).

Symmachus was another Gentile who had converted and his translation was apparently more elegant than Aquila's. His work was more of a paraphrase than a literal "word-for-word" translation, giving the gist of a passage rather than an exact representation.

Theodotion could have been a Jew, a Christian, or both and produced a revision of the Septuagint, rather than a fresh translation. His translations of Job and Daniel were generally preferred at that time to the official Septuagint versions.

There was another important translator who was quite dismissive of the Septuagint. This was Jerome, a 4th century Christian living in south-eastern Europe. Now considered a Catholic saint, Jerome was commissioned by the Pope to create a translation of the Hebrew Scriptures into Latin, the language of the clergy. This became known as the *Latin Vulgate*, still influential today. Jerome learnt Hebrew from Jewish Christians in Antioch and devoted the last 34 years of his career to this massive undertaking, as well as other lesser-known works. For over a thousand years (between 400 AD and 1530 AD), the Vulgate was the most influential Bible in Western Europe, indeed it was the only Bible many ever encountered. Even today many "religious" words that we encounter, such as *creation, salvation, justification* and *sanctification*, owe their origins to this Latin tome.

Before the Vulgate, all Latin versions of the Hebrew Scriptures were produced from the Septuagint, but against all advice Jerome refused to do the same. Quite rightly, he did not consider the Septuagint in any way inspired, as it was fundamentally a translation from source material that was not the most reliable around at that time. Nevertheless, he did make some use of the *Hexapla* in his translation, so it wasn't 100% from the original Hebrew.

We have already ascertained that the framework of the Hebrew Scriptures canonised by the Jews at Yavneh was identical in content to the "Old Testament" of the Christians, the only difference being the organisation and division of the individual books, from the 24 books of the Jewish Bible to the 39 books of the Christian "Old Testament". There are exceptions, though. The Roman Catholics and Eastern Orthodox include other content that was excluded by the Jews, tagging them onto their Bible as a kind of appendix. These are the *deuterocanonical* books that Protestants term the *apocrypha*. They are not considered as having the authority of the "official" canon of Scripture though. The decision as to the order of the books to include in the "official" canon of the Christian "Old Testament" was made at a series of Church Councils in the 4th century AD.

Meanwhile the *Sopherim* were busy from generation to generation, painstakingly ensuring the purity of God's Word, as they copied it through the centuries. Nothing much happened on this front for a few hundred years, and then a lot happened all at once.

Chapter Eight

A Greek Bypass

By this time, two paths were being trod – by those *from within* who were sworn to protect God's Word in its original language and those *from without* who sought to use it to help explain their new life as Gentile followers of Jesus the Messiah. While the *Sopherim* were poring over ancient manuscripts and painstakingly going about their business, someone else was also poring over similar manuscripts for other purposes. For his story we must return to Alexandria, in Egypt, the birthplace of the *Septuagint*, to see the legacy of this significant work of translation.

The man is Philo, a Jew living around the time of Jesus. He saw the Septuagint, the translation of the *Torah* into Greek, as a major event of revelation, equal to the actual giving of the *Torah* to Moses at Mount Sinai. He saw himself as the one to open up the *Torah* to the whole Greek-speaking world ... *to the Jew first and then to the Gentiles* (where have I heard that before? Romans 1:16, actually). His own people were far from impressed, but his legacy to the Christian church was enormous ... sadly. What he did and what drove him to do so is related in my book, *How the Church Lost the Way*, which investigates the infiltration of pagan Greek philosophy into early Christianity. His mindset wavered between the Hebraic one of his ancestors and the Greek one of Plato, which emphasised the effect of *dualism*, in creating a division between the spiritual and the physical, the former being "good" and the latter "bad".

This thought process even extended to how he viewed the Hebrew Scriptures, interpreting them on two or even three levels. He looked at plain simple meanings of biblical texts, but also deeper meanings, through the use of such tools as *allegory*. These deeper meanings tended to feature in cases where he considered Scripture unworthy of God or hard for him to understand in its plain, simple sense. He was one of the first of a long line of Bible interpreters who would use their own imaginations and intellect to discern God's Word, rather than let it speak for itself.

Belonging to this tradition were the *Gnostics*, rampant *spiritualisers*, who are still very much alive and kicking today. They would have a very confused idea of the Godhead, stating that the God of the Hebrew Scriptures – a malevolent and angry person for them – was not the same as the God of the New Testament. Equally, not all Christians were the same and *only they* had the keys to the secret knowledge contained within God's Word. All this, again, was a result of allowing Plato's ideas into the church.

One such Gnostic was *Clement of Alexandria*, who also happened to be a church Father, and so historically relevant. He was greatly influenced by Philo, but took things further in declaring that there were five possible senses in which Hebrew Scripture could be interpreted: the historical sense, the doctrinal sense, the prophetic sense, the philosophical sense and the mystical sense. OK, fine, but what tools are there to process each of these senses? Clement considered the New Testament as the superior revelation and so used this to re-evaluate the *inferior* "Old Testament". It was the dualism of Plato morphing into theology, as interpreted by the intellect of the Christian philosopher.

His successor in Alexandria was *Origen*, a cleverer man and the Christian philosopher with the greatest legacy, particularly as he produced many written works, including the *Hexapla*, already mentioned in the last chapter. His approach to theology and Bible interpretation was documented in his book, *De Principiis*. He saw the purpose of Holy Scripture as a "man-centred" thing, centring on our desire for *intellectual truths*, rather than God revealing himself to us and acting in human history. He provided thousands of examples in the "Old Testament" where he felt free to spiritualise and allegorise God's Word.

For instance, he dissected much that was in the Creation account in Genesis, arguing against any literal interpretations of such events as the first three days of Creation, the trees in the Garden of Eden or God actually walking in the garden. All were allegorised, explained away as stories with deeper spiritual meanings dreamt up by his own intellect. Here is his approach, in his own words:

> *The exact reader will hesitate in regard to some passages, finding himself unable to decide without considerable investigation whether a particular incident, believed to be history, actually happened or not. Accordingly he who reads in an exact manner must, in obedience to the Saviour's precept which says, "Search the scriptures" (John 5:39), carefully investigate how far the literal meaning is true and how far it is impossible, and to the utmost of his power must trace out from the use of similar expressions the meaning scattered everywhere throughout the scriptures of that which when taken literally is impossible.*

(De Principiis 4.3.5)

To Origen, all was spiritual and not all was literal. He believed that there were spiritual, symbolic meanings for *all Scripture*. It's just up to certain cleverer people to discern what these are and then tell the rest! This, to me, is not consistent with the God I know, who reminds us of the Hebrew Scriptures, in 2 Timothy 3:14–17:

> *But as for you, continue in what you have learned and have become convinced of, because you know those from whom you learned it,and how from infancy you have known the Holy Scriptures, which are able to make you wise for salvation through faith in Christ Jesus. All Scripture is God-breathed and is useful for teaching, rebuking, correcting and training in righteousness,so that the man of God may be thoroughly equipped for every good work.*

God's Word is *for all*, not just trained Greek Christian philosophers. So we have briefly travelled on a Greek bypass, a ring road around the centrality of God's revelation. These Greek Gentile church Fathers were all basing their teachings on what was basically a *translation*, not the original material. The *Septuagint* had already been rejected by the Jews by the 3rd or 4th century AD, and even many of the Gentile scholars were starting to find holes in it. But, Jerome aside, there were few real Hebrew scholars in the Christian world and so they found themselves reading and writing God's Word in Greek, and basically dissecting and analysing it using Greek techniques.

But not all Gentiles were butchering the Hebrew Scriptures. In the Eastern part of the Empire, in Antioch, there were some who viewed God's Word with a lot more care. This was because of the Jewish element that was influential well into the 3rd century AD, ensuring that Greek techniques did not infiltrate the work of theologians there. In fact some of them wrote specifically against Origen. They insisted on the historical reality of biblical revelation, unwilling to see it sinking into a mire of symbolism and allegory.

It is time to leave the bypass and return to Hebrew-ville.

Chapter Nine

The Masoretic Explosion

There is a group of Jews who have been around for over a thousand years, who have been known by many labels, from a *fringe sect* to a *movement of biblical revival*. These are the *Karaites*, a word taking the meaning "Readers of the Hebrew Scriptures". You couldn't get a plainer title, you couldn't get a nobler title, yet it has always stirred up a whole gamut of emotions from among the religious Jewish community. This is because they are *just* "readers of the Hebrew Scriptures", to them everything else is *not* from God. In other words they have never had any time for anything the Rabbis may have written, including the *Talmud*, *Mishnah*, *Midrashim*, *Targumim* and the plethora of commentaries and discourses that have poured forth from learned Jewish minds, *allegedly* since Moses received an oral tradition as well as a written tradition as he chatted with God on Mount Sinai.

One of the first prominent *Karaites* was Aaron ben Moses ben Asher, historically and certainly in the context of our story, a *very* important man. He was the last of his line to take up the family business, that of compiling what has since become the earliest and most authoritative version of the Scriptures in Hebrew. Being a *Karaite* must have helped, ensuring no distractions from anything that wasn't of acknowledged divine origin.

He was one of the *Masoretes*, super-scribes. How we view these men depends on our perspective. Were they heroes or villains? We need to make our mind up about this and we will follow this plotline a little later on, once we've found out more about them and their work.

We first start hearing about them at around the 8th century AD. By this time, it was becoming clear that, although the scribes had ensured that the text of the Hebrew Scriptures was being faithfully reproduced, the reading of the text was problematic. After all, it was all in consonants and people were not too sure of the pronunciations any more, as there was no written standardisation. Basically, the text was crying out for vowels to be added!

One of the first men to do something about this was Asher the Elder, who started to add *accents*, which indicated which letters to stress in any word and where there should be pauses, as well as vowel points. Asher was the first of five generations of *Masoretes* in his family, the *ben Asher* family. They lived and worked in Tiberias. The last of their family was Aaron ben Asher, the *Karaite*, the most well-known and influential of all *Masoretes*. He worked on what has become the most important manuscript of the Hebrew Scriptures, used ever since as a principal template for many modern Bibles. This is the *Leningrad Codex*, completed in 1008 AD. This is now the oldest complete manuscript of the Hebrew Scriptures in Hebrew and can be found in the National Library of Russia, in St Petersburg, if you fancy a visit.

So what about these vowels, then? Well, these were basically a series of dots and symbols mostly placed underneath the letters. Here's a short summary of the important ones:

The A sound
Short vowel (as in b<u>a</u>d) = ▬
Long vowel (as in f<u>a</u>ther) = ⲧ

The E sound
Short vowel (as in b<u>e</u>d) = ⁖
Long vowel (as in h<u>e</u>y) = ▬▬

The I sound
Short vowel (as in b<u>i</u>d) = •

The O sound
Long vowel (as in h<u>o</u>le) = ֹו

The U sound
Short vowel (as in p<u>u</u>t) = ֻ

But there are variations. Just as England boasts a variety of dialects and regional accents, there are two historical traditions in Hebrew speech, depending on whether the speaker is an *Ashkenazi* Jew (mostly German or Polish origin) or a *Sephardi* Jew (mostly Spanish origin). I was brought up in the *Ashkenazi* tradition, and for me the main difference has been in the pronunciation of the words *Shabbat* (Sabbath) and *Succot* (Tabernacles). The first I was brought up to pronounce as "Shobbos" and the second as "Succos". Here's why: The *Ashkenazi* tradition quite often pronounces the *tav* as an "s" sound, whereas it's always a "t" sound with the *Sephardis*. The vowel "e" (long) is pronounced "ai" rather than "e". The vowel "a" (long) is pronounced "o" (as in "dot") rather than "a". So *Ashkenazis* would say "Dovid" rather than "David" and "Omayn" rather than "Amen". These days it's the *Sephardi* pronunciations that hold sway both in Israel and in Biblical Hebrew classes, so I need to retrain my vowels!

Let's now have a look again at a couple of the Hebrew words we have met so far.

Firstly, the word for shepherd, *ro'eh*:

רעה (resh – ayin – hey)

Of course this has no vowels. Ancient Hebrews knew how to pronounce this without needing vowels to be printed and so do we now, thanks to the Masoretes. Here is the full word, with vowels:

רֹעֶה

The dot above the *ayin* signifies a long "o" sound and the three dots below it signify a short "e" sound. So we get r – o – e – h.

Then there is *torah*, the word for "teaching or instruction":

תורה (tav – vav – resh – hey)

Here is the full word, with vowels:

תּוֹרָה

The dot above the vav turns it into a vowel (a Hebrew quirk) and produces a long "o" sound and the symbol below the resh signifies a long "a" sound. So we get t – o – r – a – h.

But what about the sacred name of God? What did the *Masoretes* do when they saw this name (also called the *tetragrammaton*)?

יהוה

It was the name never to be pronounced. But the *Masoretes'* job was to add vowels to all words and make them *pronounceable*. Were they going to go against centuries of Jewish tradition? Well, they added vowels. This is what they ended up with:

יְהֹוָה

So, bearing in mind that this was the *unpronounceable* name, why did they add vowels and why *those* particular vowels? Therein lies a story. What the *Masoretes* wanted to do was, in fact, make sure that readers *didn't* accidentally say the sacred name, so they purposely put the *wrong* vowels in! At that point in history, anyone reading the name יהוה would have automatically substituted it with another word, the word for *Lord*. This is the word:

אדני (aleph – dalet – nun – yod)

And here it is with its full complement of vowels:

אֲדֹנָי = ADONAI

So, to remind readers to say אדני when they saw יהוה they took the *vowels* for *adonai* and used them on the sacred name, producing:

יְהֹוָה

Of course this is Hebrew and nothing is ever cut and dried and so you will notice that the last two vowels follow this rule, but the first doesn't. There is nothing sinister going on here, it's just due to a law in Hebrew grammar, which states what vowels can appear under which letter. So what we have here is the best fit, something that the readers would have understood.

What happened next? Let's move forwards to the early English translators of the Bible. Without going into complex detail, these men were unaware of what the *Masoretes* had done and also had no fear themselves about uttering the sacred name, so they translated *exactly* what they saw.

יְהֹוָה   (Y – e – H – o – V – a – H)

And thus a new name for God was produced, an *incorrect* one. The rest, as they say, is history. This would be a surprise to the *Jehovah*'s Witnesses and other groups who use this name for God and could be a useful conversation starter when opening a discussion with them.

What of today? What is the acceptable attitude today among Christians? Are we bound by the sensibilities of those Jews who declared that the name of God was unutterable or do we attempt to say his name, but at least *get it right*?

The vast majority of Bibles, whether Jewish or Christian, continue to use the word LORD (*Adonai*) in the text. Orthodox Jews today *never* write the name "God" or even "Lord", and replace the vowel with a hyphen, writing it thus, "G–d" or "L–rd". In speech they use other terms. A popular one is *Ha Shem* (the name). There is even one used by Matthew, the Gospel writer specifically writing to the Jewish people of his day. When speaking of the Kingdom that Jesus had come to initiate, all other writers used the expression "Kingdom of God". In Matthew's case, although he used this expression four times, he used another one 34 times, the only Gospel writer to do so. He used the expression *Kingdom of Heaven*. This avoided using the word "God" and used instead the euphemism *Heaven*.

Many scholars and Christians today, when they want to say the name of God and demonstrate their knowledge of Hebrew, tend to use the name *Yahweh*. Where does that come from? It seems from a 19th century German rationalist and Bible critic called Wilhelm Gesenius. Not a good start, with something of such importance to the faith community coming from the mind of a rational scholar. The way I see it, this cannot be correct, just from one of the simplest facts of Hebrew grammar, the pronunciation of the letters. Let's have another look at the consonants:

יהוה

No problem with the first two, יה, as they could feasibly pronounce the name YAH (Yod – a – Hey), in fact YAH, particularly as a suffix or prefix, is all over the Hebrew Scriptures, with "God" as a meaning. A good example is *Hallelu – yah* (Praise God). But the third letter is a problem. It is a *vav* and gives a "v" sound. It never gives a "w" sound. So how did they end up with Yahweh and not Yahveh? Heaven knows!

The reason why Jews don't say the sacred name is their take on the Third Commandment:

> "*You shall not misuse the name of the* LORD *your God, for the* LORD *will not hold anyone guiltless who misuses his name*" (Exodus 20:7).

The question we Christians need to ask is how do we use his name? If we are sincerely calling out to him, worshipping him or referring to him reverentially, then I can't see what is wrong in using his name: God Almighty. But too many of us do misuse his name, using his name in vain. Every time we use his name in a sentence ended by an exclamation mark, we are mocking him! The church used to call it *blasphemy* and there used to be laws against it. Ignore the pay-off line of the Third Commandment – *for the* LORD *will not hold anyone guiltless who misuses his name*– at your peril.

———————

So the *Masoretes* fixed a definitive version of God's Word (thus initiating a new chain of custody) and ensured that the words could now be read (and sung) in a standardised way. They also divided the text into verses and sections. But they did more. Out of their love of God and zeal for his Word, they wanted to ensure that any future readers and copyists would not fall into any error or misunderstanding of the sacred text. They wanted to preserve the integrity of every letter of every word, serving as a fence around the Holy Scripture. Although they added the vowels and other marks, they never altered a single letter of Hebrew that was passed down to them. If they wished to draw attention to any Hebrew text they did this through the *Masorah*.

Think of *Masorah* as study aids. These are notes added to the main text, whether on side margins, or in the header or footer, or at the end of the manuscript. They are written mostly in Aramaic, but also in Hebrew. They provide guidelines regarding letters, words or phrases wherever there is a possibility of error. Their work would have guarded against such things as the omissions of letters or words, unwarranted repetitions, reversals of letters or words and any other errors of the eye. But they did much more than that, they really created the world's first study Bible.

What the *Masoretes* basically did was lay down the fundamentals for the hypertext system that was to reach its fulfilment in the development of the internet over a thousand years later! To help you appreciate this, here's an example. It's a good one, it's the first word in the Hebrew Scriptures, in Genesis 1:1:

בראשית*(bet – resh–aleph – shin–yod– tav)* = bereshit =*In the beginning.*

This word is linked to a note in the left-hand margin – this is called the *masorah parva*. The note is made up of twelve marks, mostly Hebrew letters, but also numbers and punctuation marks. The first is the letter *hey* (ה), which, if you remember, also represents the number 5. This is telling us that the word בראשית appears five times in all. Then a *gimmel* (ג) tells us that this Hebrew word appears three (the numerical equivalent of a gimmel) times at the start of a verse. Next to the gimmel is a number 1. This links to footnotes at the bottom, the *masorah magna*, which again links to a separate volume, the *masorah gedolah*, which lists these occurrences. Finally there is a bet (ב), which tells us that the Hebrew word appears twice (bet = 2) within a verse. Next to this bet is a number 2, which links to a second footnote in the *masorah magna*, which in turn links to the *masorah gedolah*, which lists these two occurrences. This is just on the *first* word of the Bible. And they did all this without computers! Now, perhaps, we can appreciate their dedicated hard work.

The *Masoretes* are particularly vigilant anywhere the name of God is mentioned. Sometimes their zeal can seem a bit extreme. Here's an example. If you go to Genesis 18:22 in any Bible, you read this:

> *The men turned away and went toward Sodom, but Abraham remained standing before the* LORD.

If you have an NIV Bible and look at the footnotes for this verse, you see the following:

> *Masoretic Text: but the Lord remained standing before Abraham.*

What this tells us is that, in the original Hebrew Scriptures, as passed down from generation to generation from Ezra onwards (all corresponding to God's Word as written down by Moses), the *actual* text says:

> *The men turned away and went toward Sodom, but the*
> LORD *remained standing before Abraham.*

It appears that the Masoretes actually changed the Hebrew words because, in their eyes, it was not proper to speak of God standing in the presence of his creation. This is called an *emendation* ("alteration by editorial criticism, as of a text so as to give a better reading") of the text and the specific process of doing this to the Hebrew Scriptures is called a *tikkun Sopherim*. They may have made the change, but they still preserved the original wording and added a full commentary as to what they had done through the *Masorah* footnotes, with the marker *Tiq soph* (*tikkun sopherim*).

There are another seventeen passages in the Hebrew Scriptures that have been *emended* by scribes for theological reasons, all for the best reasons, their utter devotion to God. These are in the following passages: Numbers 11:15, 12:12; 1 Samuel 3:13; 2 Samuel 16:12, 20:1; 1 Kings 12:16; 2 Chronicles 10:16; Jeremiah 2:11; Ezekiel 8:17; Hosea 4:7; Habakkuk 1:12; Zechariah 2:12; Malachi 1:13; Psalm 106:20; Job 7:20, 32:3 and Lamentations 3:20. All are far too subtle for our untrained eyes, involving the swapping of single Hebrew letters.

Then there are other oddities, such as suspended letters. On just four occasions, a Hebrew letter is written higher than it should be. The first is in Judges 18:30:

> *There the Danites set up for themselves the idols, and Jonathan son of Gershom, the son of Moses, and his sons were priests for the tribe of Dan until the time of the captivity of the land.*

Here a letter *nun* (נ) is suspended above the name of Moses. The only reason for this was the reverence the *Masoretes* had for Moses. They wanted to spare him the bad reputation of having a dodgy priest for a grandson! Rather than totally destroy their reputation for impartiality by inserting the letter "n" and changing Moses into *Manasseh*, they just left this extra letter hanging there, perhaps hoping it may drop of its own accord! What a hoot! (Interestingly, the King James Version, unaware of this scenario, includes the word *Manasseh*, despite it not making sense.)

The other three suspended letters are all *ayins* (ע). The first, in Psalm 80:14, seems to be added to call attention to what is the middle letter in the Psalms. The other two are both in Job, chapter 38, in verses 13 and 15. There seems to be mixed opinion as to the reasons for this, the general consensus indicates a minor correction to the text.

Then there is the *inverted nun*, notably after Numbers 10:34 and Numbers 10:36. The purpose was to draw attention to verses 35 and 36, to *bracket them off*, so to speak. Here's the passage in question:

> *Whenever the ark set out, Moses said, "Rise up, O LORD! May your enemies be scattered; may your foes flee before you." Whenever it came to rest, he said, "Return, O LORD, to the countless thousands of Israel."*

The reason for doing this is because there was some doubt whether these two verses were in the correct position, something that seems to be confirmed by the Septuagint.

There are four places where letters are larger than they should be. We have already seen two of them, the enlarged ע and ד in the *Shema* (Deuteronomy 6:4), the most important prayer in Judaism. These two letters spell out the word, *ed*, taking the meaning of "witness", highlighting the need for this prayer to be a witness or a testimony to our God. Another enlarged letter is the ו (vav) in Leviticus 11:42, in the following word:

גחון

This letter is in fact the middle letter in the whole *Torah*. Apparently the *Sopherim* were hot on such things. There is one other large letter, in Numbers 27:5, but the meaning for this has been lost.

Here's another oddity in Genesis 33:4:

> *But Esau ran to meet Jacob and embraced him; he threw his*
> *arms around his neck and kissed him. And they wept.*

The word for "... *and kissed him*" is:

וַיִּשָּׁקֵהוּ

But this word, in the Masoretic text, has a dot above every letter.
The reasons for this have been lost in antiquity, it is traced back
to the early *Sopherim*, and the *Masoretes* admit that they are
clueless on this. Some have suggested that it was to indicate that
the kiss was insincere. Others have suggested that Esau didn't
kiss Jacob, but *bit him* instead, the dots representing his teeth!

To fully enter the world of the *Masoretes* would take a lifetime,
but you should now have an appreciation of what made these people tick and what a massive contribution they made to the Bibles
we read today. But some people are still not happy. ...

Chapter Ten

Can we trust these men?

So, the Masoretic text, can we trust it? Or, rather, should we say, the *Masoretes*, can we trust them? There are some who say that we can't, so it is wise for us to examine their concerns first. A clue is in their very name – "tradition keepers" – implying the necessity for the preservation of *tradition*. What "tradition" is being referred to here?

It wasn't the Jewish tradition that they were keen to preserve. Remember that the key *Masorete*, Aaron ben Moses ben Asher, was a *Karaite*, the group who certainly *weren't* in the business of preserving Jewish traditions.

Well it certainly *wasn't* the Christian tradition, and there's the rub. Living at a time when Jews were being severely persecuted by the "Christian" church on the basis of the very Scriptures that the Jews had given to the world, one would imagine that the *Masoretes* weren't over-inclined to do any favours for the church. In fact, a cynical mind would expect that they would do their utmost to sabotage the church and, as custodians of the sacred Hebrew Scripture they had the ammunition at their disposal to wreak havoc. Of course it would have to be subtle as the fruit of their labour was always going to be scrutinised by learned scholars, purists who would have very little patience with any tampering with the text, whatever the motive.

There are some in the Christian church who are prepared to accept the worst, perhaps because that's what they would have done if they had been 10th century Jewish scribes.

There was only one tradition that was worthy to be preserved and that was God's tradition, encapsulated in *God's Word*.

Now, I repeat my question: the *Masoretes* – *heroes or villains?*
We've already seen the reality of minor tampering with the text,
the *tikkun sopherim*. We must examine the motives behind this,
and they do seem to be for the best of reasons, their devotion to
God and their desire not to see his name lessened or compro-
mised in the text. Also their actions really do seem like an honest
endeavour to preserve God's Word and, even when they were
confronted by a tricky passage, word or even letter, they resisted
the temptation to tamper with the text and, when they did make
suggestions, the original text was still visible to the reader. The
Masoretic text was to become the definitive "Old Testament"
script source in Christian Bibles, and was to become for Jews *the*
Hebrew Scriptures, passed down in unaltered form as the *Tenach*
you will find in synagogues throughout the world today.

There are three questions we Christians need to ask, I believe,
if we *really* take our faith seriously:

1. Do we believe in a God who would allow his words to be
   incorrectly recorded? i.e., Do we accept that the text of the
   Bible is 100% inspired by God?
2. Do we believe in a God who would allow his words to be
   incorrectly arranged? i.e., Do we accept that the collection
   of books that have become the "Old Testament" and "New
   Testament" are what God ordained them to be?
3. Do we believe in a God who would allow his words to be
   incorrectly transmitted? i.e., Do we accept that those responsible for copying the text have got it right?

If we are prepared to accept the standard answers for Christians
on the first two questions, then we must also be prepared to accept
that, although the *Masoretes* could have had a sinister agenda in
altering Scripture to try and discredit the church, we must have sufficient faith to believe that they didn't. So, in conclusion, I would
judge the *Masoretes* as *heroes*, purists who had ample opportunity
to become villains, but who resisted the "dark side".

Another question will need to be asked a bit later concerning those responsible for translating the original texts into other

languages. Did God always have his hand on them in the same way as he had on the original writers (Moses, Ezra, etc), scribes (Ezra, Masoretes, etc) and those who set the Canon of the Old and New Testament (Council of Yavneh, church councils, etc)?

Those of the "Greek" mindset thought very differently about all of this and we have already read of the fruits of their labours – Higher Criticism and all that flowed from it. Doubts increased yearly from the mid-19th century thanks to these scholars. Their progress was relentless as they chipped away at the integrity of God's Word. That is until 1947, when their world began to collapse around them. That was the year when the Dead Sea Scrolls were first discovered.

This was a major discovery of more than 200 biblical manuscripts in all, including every book of the Hebrew Bible except Esther and Song of Songs. Among the Hebrew manuscripts found were what are believed to be the source texts for both the Septuagint and the Masoretic text, which helped to explain why there were some differences between them. Among these scrolls was what is known as the Isaiah scroll, a virtually complete version of the Bible book of that name. You can see this scroll if you visit the *Shrine of the Book*, part of the Israel Museum in Jerusalem. It is there as the central exhibit, in its entirety, all twenty-four feet of it. This scroll dates back to a time well before Jesus, in fact to around 100 BC, the time of the *Sopherim* and the Great Assembly. It would have been created by a *Sopher*, copied according to the exacting rules set by Ezra, probably from a master scroll from the Jerusalem Temple. It is by far the oldest copy of the book of Isaiah known to exist. Before 1947, the oldest known copy of the Book of Isaiah was contained in the *Leningrad Codex* mentioned earlier, created in 1008 AD by the Ben Asher *Masoretes* in Tiberias. So the Bible scholars did the obvious and compared these two manuscripts, one 1100 years older than the other one. It was reported that out of just 166 words from Isaiah a mere seventeen letters raised a question, of which most (ten) were just spelling issues, with another four being minor matters of style, whilst the other three letters concerned a single word that didn't much affect the meaning. So after some ten centuries of the text being handed down, there was only a question about a single word, and that didn't have much impact on the sense! (For fuller information, see Norman Geisler and William Nix, *A General Introduction to the Bible*, Moody Press, p.263).

There is a general consensus of a 98% agreement between the two manuscripts. The remaining 2% of deviation is said to be explained by spelling errors, scribal omissions and insertions. Yes, there are differences, the odd spelling mistake and minor corruption. We humans are not 100% infallible and despite the exacting rules and regulations set for copying manuscripts by the *Sopherim* and the *Masoretes*, they were not going to get it 100% correct. Moses had it 100%, as did every original writer of Holy Scripture, but once men started copying from those original documents, errors would be unavoidable. That accounts for the 2% deviation between the Dead Sea Isaiah scroll and the Leningrad Codex. We should not allow it to concern us, it has been proven that this 2% is not in critical verses. But there's more. Do you honestly believe that our God would take the trouble of inspiring his word to be transmitted to us and then allowing our fallibilities to obscure it, even corrupt it? Of course not, despite what the Muslims say about the Bible being altered significantly over time.

We find that the vast majority of modern Jewish and Christian Bibles depend on the Masoretic text as an accurate account of what Moses, Ezra and the others wrote down as God's Word, though, as we shall find later on, in the case of Christian "Old Testament" translations, scholars would reference the Septuagint in places where they felt compelled to disagree with the Masoretic text. But here's an interesting thought. Although we ascribe a late date to the Masoretic text, in view of the fact that the *Masoretes* themselves lived in the 9th–11th centuries, the source material is believed to pre-date the Hebrew Scriptures used in the Septuagint translation around a thousand years earlier! This source is known by scholars as the *proto-Masoretic text*. Let me explain.

We have already followed the chain of custody of the earliest texts of the Hebrew Scriptures, as produced by Ezra and the early *Sopherim*. It is believed that that very text was the basis for the

Masoretic text, the source material that was going to be so faithfully copied over the next thousand years or so, and that there would be only the slightest of variations once it was to reach the hands of the *Masoretes*. On the other hand, the source material that ended up in Egypt and was to be used to produce the Septuagint was, at some point, diverted away from the *Masoretic* line of *Sopherim*, creating a new chain of custody, which wasn't as scrupulously observed as the other one. Admittedly this is all guesswork (by clever scholars), but the fact remains that there have to be some explanations for the differences between the Septuagint and the Masoretic versions of God's Word.

This *proto-Masoretic* text still had to be preserved during turbulent times. When Jerusalem fell in 70 AD, the text was smuggled to the academy at Yavneh, but also appeared at other important centres of Jewish scholarship, such as Tiberias, and also in the academies in Babylon. From this point onwards, the text was guarded and revered by the sages, who rejected all other versions of the Hebrew Scriptures, such as the Septuagint and the Samaritan Pentateuch. It is amazing that this same Hebrew text has survived intact countless centuries and I have been privileged recently to benefit from the fruits of this incredible dedication.

———————

For a Jew today, reading the Holy Scriptures in Hebrew, it is simple: they would be reading the unexpurgated, untouched *Masoretic* text, the exact words as produced by the *Masoretes* over a thousand years earlier. It is the same with the *sefer Torah*, the scrolls read in any synagogue today. The only difference, it seems, is that only in book form are the vowels included – if you read from the *sefer Torah* you are expected to know the pronunciation of the words already! Let me now tell you of my two encounters with a *sefer Torah*.

The first time was in a crowded, noisy synagogue, packed with relatives. Ladies with hats in the gallery, grey-suited men with *kippas* clipped to whatever hair remained, in the stalls. It was my *barmitzvah*, the day I had sacrificed two hours every Tuesday evening for, over four years. Wedged between the rabbis and (I think) my dad, the scrolls loomed before me, flaunting an angry sea of Hebrew letters, as I nervously clutched the pointer and launched into my (very short-lived) Hebrew singing career with a wavering stutter.

The second time was very different! It was in the small empty meeting room of *Beit Sar Shalom*, a Messianic fellowship in North London. Again I stood before the *sefer Torah*, the sacred handwritten scrolls of the five books of Moses. But this time there was no tension in the air, no dryness of the throat or knotting in the guts, no atmosphere of anticipation, just a primal wonder and reverence for God's Word in its rawest form. I was alone, just me and the scrolls, a wonderful privilege granted to me by Daniel Nessim, the congregational leader. These were of *Sephardi* origin, around 150 years old, from the Jewish community in Morocco. Daniel slipped them out of the ornately decorated blue velvet cover and placed the scrolls gingerly on the desk in front of me. *It's all yours.*

A moment passed. By today's standards of presentation they weren't much to look at: a continuous stream of Hebrew letters on a strangely translucent and waxy parchment, stitched together in panels and attached to a pair of wooden rollers. The parchment had once been the skin of a *kosher* animal, which had also provided the stitching through its hair, and even the quill pen which the scribe used to create the lettering. Everything so minimalist and plain. Just God's Word transmitted from a living human being to another, through the medium of a dead animal.

This particular *sefer Torah* had seen better days (a matter of opinion, I suppose, considering the sad history of the Jews). The lettering was faded in places – in some instances there was some retouching. There were stains, smudges, the odd hole and even some over-zealous pencil marks. It was all so real, so raw, so authentic. Of course all 304,805 letters were created by hand by a *Sopher* (a tradition now well over 2,000 years old) who had to be meticulous in his work. Any mistake had to be scraped away, unless it was the name of God, in which case the page was scrapped and a new one stitched in its place. The scrolls that lay before me would be deemed *non-kosher* by an orthodox synagogue, by virtue of their lived-in state, but it was good enough for me, *more* than good enough.

It was as if God had downloaded his mind in one fell swoop, pouring out his instructions to his people in a continuous string of holy letters. In our over-designed computer age, where everything is indexed, annotated, linked and numbered, this would be laughed at and discarded by any discerning consumer. After all, what good is a string of letters (without vowels), barely arranged as discernible words, without headings or consistent verse or chapter divisions? *It may be God's way of speaking his mind, but he could have made it easier, couldn't he?* Of course, that's just our perspective, in our hurried "sound-bite" culture, and quite sad really.

I rolled back the scroll to the beginning, so at least I could have a point of reference, Genesis, chapter 1, verse 1. Again I couldn't get the rawness of it out of my mind. We are so used to design and colour and context. Where was the Preface, the Introduction, the handy Index and list of contents? No, just a bit of ragged stitching, then straight into the text:

בראשית ברא אלהים את השמים ואת הארץ

The words of God, as written by a Moroccan Jew in the mid-19th century, copied letter by letter from an earlier scroll, which itself would have been produced in the same painstaking way, the latest in a long line going right back for hundreds and hundreds of years. Those are the first words of Genesis, so familiar to those of us who claim to have just a smidgeon of Hebrew and are seemingly too exhausted or perplexed to go any further than those first seven words of the Hebrew Scriptures. We, of course, are going to go *a lot further* in this book. I followed through the text that lay before me, with a copy of the Hebrew Scriptures as reference, i.e. one with verse numbering, vowels and an English translation. I was able to make a few observations.

- There may not have been vowels, but the text did have markings, known as *accents*, though it seems there is not a consistent agreement as to how these should be used.

- The text was right- and left-justified, meaning that some letters, particularly near the end of a line, were elongated, to make the words fit. I was keen to discover whether there were any other reasons for this elongation, or whether it represented a degree of leeway on the part of the scribe.
- The text was arranged in blocks, similar to our paragraph divisions. But it didn't equate to the verse and chapter divisions that we are used to. For instance, the first block had the first five verses of Genesis chapter 1; the second block had the next three verses, etc.

This brings up an important point, worth investigating I think. We must bear in mind that the chapters and verse divisions that we are used to in Holy Scripture were produced by scholars and were not included, hinted at or alluded to in the original text. If the *Torah* scroll is displaying text in a different way, then perhaps we must sit up and take notice. On this same point I noticed that, on the *Torah* scroll, Genesis chapter 2 and chapter 3 just flow into each other. If someone felt it important enough to divide these up into chapters, why didn't the authors of the *Torah* scrolls ... or, should I say, *Author*? There was plenty of food for thought in my brief scroll encounter.

Chapter Eleven
What about the English?

Of course not all Jews read Hebrew fluently and so there are translations into English, perhaps the most popular being the one published by the Jewish Publication Society (JPS). It is insightful to read some extracts from the Preface to the 1917 edition, regarding the need for an English translation of the "Old Testament" to be produced by Jews rather than Christian Gentiles. First they explain their reasons:

> *The present translation is the first for which a group of men representative of Jewish learning among English-speaking Jews assume joint responsibility, all previous efforts in the English language having been the work of individual translators. It has a character of its own. It aims to combine the spirit of Jewish tradition with the results of biblical scholarship, ancient, medieval, and modern. It gives to the Jewish world a translation of the Scriptures done by men imbued with the Jewish consciousness, while the non-Jewish world, it is hoped, will welcome a translation that presents many passages from the Jewish traditional point of view.*

Then they offer gratitude to those Christians who have already undertaken the task of translating *their* Scriptures into English:

> *The repeated efforts by Jews in the field of biblical translation show their sentiment toward translations prepared by other denominations. The dominant feature of this sentiment, apart from the thought that the christological*

interpretations in non-Jewish translations are out of place in a Jewish Bible, is and was that the Jew cannot afford to have his Bible translation prepared for him by others. He cannot have it as a gift, even as he cannot borrow his soul from others. If a new country and a new language metamorphose him into a new man, the duty of this new man is to prepare a new garb and a new method of expression for what is most sacred and most dear to him. We are, it is hardly needful to say, deeply grateful for the works of our non-Jewish predecessors, such as the Authorised Version with its admirable diction, which can never be surpassed, as well as for the Revised Version with its ample learning – but they are not ours.

Finally, they declare their methodology:

As to the text and order of the biblical books, the present translation follows Jewish tradition, the Sacred Scriptures having come down in a definite compass and in a definite text. They are separated into three divisions: Law (Torah, Pentateuch), Prophets (Nebi'im), Writings (Ketubim). Each of these possesses a different degree of holiness or authority. In the Prophets and the Writings the order of the books varies in manuscripts or among Jewish authorities; but there is absolute agreement as to the compass of these two divisions, and no book is transposed from the one into the other. Thus Ruth, Lamentations, and Daniel are all placed in the division of Writings – not among the Prophets, as in non-Jewish versions.

With every step by which each of the three parts was sealed, nothing to be added or to be taken away, the text was likewise fixed and thenceforth made the object of zealous watchfulness. Even with regard to the latest book of our Scriptures, we read its text substantially in the form in which the great Rabbi Akiba read it, he who said that the system by which the sacred text was guarded constituted a fence about the Scriptures. In that system, at first oral and later committed to writing, the letters were actually counted and lists made, to the end that no alterations should creep in at the hands of careless scribes.

Up until this point, Jews have had to make do with "Christian" translations of the Hebrew Scriptures, such as the King James Version. It made perfect sense to have an English version of their own Scriptures and it will be interesting to compare this translation with the Christian "Old Testament" versions, to see what we can learn.

So we now turn our thoughts to English. Before we focus on the 16th century, let's go back in time a very long way, to a time when there wasn't a written English language at all. It's the 7th century AD and missionaries brought the Latin alphabet to these shores, from which came English and most other European alphabets. This Latin alphabet had in turn been adapted from the Greek alphabet many centuries earlier, along with their religion, philosophy and culture. And what about the Greek alphabet? Let me tell you a story.

You will remember that Biblical Hebrew was derived from an earlier form of Hebrew, called *Phoenician-Old Hebrew.* The Phoenicians were seafaring traders, operating in the Mediterranean region. They traded with the Greeks, and legend tells us that one day a Phoenician conducted a transaction with a Greek and insisted that a record be made of the sale. The Greek was unable because, to the amazement of the other, he couldn't write, because there was no such thing as a Greek alphabet!

"Show me how", was the anguished cry and the Phoenician showed him how he did it. He showed him the twenty-two letters of his alphabet and the sounds they described. So off the Greek went and conferred with others and out of this came a process resulting in the Greek alphabet, based on the Phoenician alphabet (and, by implication, the Hebrew alphabet). All was well and good, but one day the Greek met up with the Phoenician again and said,

"Where are the vowel signs in your alphabet? We need them or we can't write our Greek words properly."

"Well, we don't need them," replied the other, "we get on OK without them."

It turned out that Greek simply couldn't be written down without separate letters for vowels. So they looked again at the *Phoenician-Old Hebrew* alphabet and identified five letters that were not needed for Greek words and converted them into *vowel* letters. So the ayin (ע) became an "o" sound, the aleph (א) became an "a", the hey (ה) became an "e", the chet (ח) became an "ay" sound and the yod (י) became an "ee" sound.

And from this development, all European languages, from English to Russian, have separate letters as vowel sounds, separating them from the Semitic languages such as Hebrew, which use vowel points instead. The other difference is the direction of writing. Why is Hebrew written backwards (right to left)?

Actually, there are a few possible answers. There's a mystical reason that suggests that the *right* side indicates greater spiritual revelation than the *left* side. There's a practical reason, dating back to the earliest uses of the earliest form of the language (Canaanite), when the letters were chiselled out of stone. It is simply more comfortable for right-handed people to chisel from right to left. Try it and see! Perhaps a better question to ask is why the Greeks changed the direction of writing.

Let's see how this transition from the Hebrew letters to European letters was achieved.

From the *aleph* (א), came the Greek *alpha*, now a vowel, eventually becoming the English "a".

From the *bet* (ב), came the Greek *beta*, then the English "b".

From the *gimmel* (ג) came the Greek *gamma*, a "g" sound. The Etruscans used this for their "c" sound and the Romans used it for both their "c" and "g" sound, eventually creating two letters, becoming the English "c" and "g".

From the *dalet* (ד) came the Greek *delta*, eventually becoming the English "d".

From the *hey* (ה), came the Greek *epsilon*, a vowel sound, eventually becoming the English "e".

From the *vav* (ו) came the Greek letters *upsilon* and *digamma*. From these came the English letters "v", "f", "w" and "u".

From the *zayin* (ז) came the Greek letter *zeta*, becoming the English "z".

From the *chet* (ח) came the Greek letter *eta*, becoming the English "h".

From the *tet* (ט) came the Greek letter *theta* but it never made it into the English alphabet.

From the *yod* (י) came the Greek letter *iota*, becoming the English "y".

From the *kaph* (כ) came the Greek letter *kappa*, finally becoming the English "k".

From the *lamed* (ל) came the Greek letter *lambda*, finally becoming the English "l".

From the *mem* (מ) came the Greek letter *mu*, finally becoming the English "m".

From the *nun* (נ) came the Greek letter *nu*, finally becoming the English "n".

From the *samech* (ס) came the Greek letter *xi* but never made it into the English alphabet.

From the *ayin* (ע) came the Greek *omikron*, a vowel sound, eventually becoming the English "o".

From the *pey* (פ) came the Greek letter *pi*, finally becoming the English "p".

The *tsade* (צ) never made it into the Greek or English alphabet.

From the *qoph* (ק) came the Greek letter *koppa*, finally becoming the English "q".

From the *resh* (ר) came the Greek letter *rho*, finally becoming the English "r".

From the *shin* (ש) came the Greek letter *sigma*, finally becoming the English "s".

From the *tav* (ת) came the Greek letter *tau*, finally becoming the English "t".

So now we have the English alphabet, let's see it in use.

Let us return to the 16th century, to the English church, that read and wrote in English, from left to right, and we turn our thoughts to the English Christian versions of the "Old Testament". We ask: *what source documents did they use?*

So we ask that question of the King James Version (KJV), the granddaddy of all English translations. There are plenty of folk around who still consider it the only authentic Bible.

Obviously, as it's now 400 years old, the accuracy of its translation of the "Old Testament" from Hebrew into English would have been according to the best scholarship available at that time.

They took, in the first instance, the Masoretic text, by way of a printed version, called *Mikraot Gedolot* (Great Scriptures), also called the "Rabbinic Bible", produced by Daniel Bomberg, a Flemish Christian, in the early 16th century. This text had already been used in a previous English "Old Testament" translation, called the *Bishops' Bible* and the actual work of translating it into the English was done by the Archbishop of Canterbury, Matthew Parker and some fellow bishops. Hence the name (though it was also called The Great English Bible). The Bishops' Bible became the chief template for the King James Version.

But this was a Bible for Christians and so they set about 'christianising' some of the text. The earlier comments in the Preface of the Jewish Publication Society Bible (*"the christological interpretations in non-Jewish translations are out of place in a Jewish Bible"*) now start to make sense. So human editors modified the plain translation of the Masoretic text, using the Greek Septuagint and the Latin Vulgate, especially in passages that seem to speak about the Messiah to come, such as Psalm 22:16 (more of that one in Chapter 15).

There were political considerations too. If the Bible was to be approved by the King, then it would have to be seen as supporting the Anglican Church, the good old Church of England. Thus the words translated as "bishop" and "church" would have to support the acceptable understanding of the *bishop* as part of the hierarchy of the state church (rather than the actual translation of the word as an elder or overseer of a local assembly) and a *church* as a building that housed this hierarchy (rather than the actual translation of the word as the called-out community of God).

There's one word, though, that the King James translators *really* messed up with subtle but dangerous consequences. That word is *Torah*. We looked at this word earlier and saw that the best way to look at it was as a set of instructions for life, for perfect living. How come the Christian world sees this word as a *negative* one, painting it as a stifling directory of laws, rules and regulations? This is how it happened....

The *Torah*, the five books of Moses, are known to us by their English names: Genesis, Exodus, Leviticus, Numbers and Deuteronomy. As we saw earlier, in the original Hebrew they are actually named according to the first word in the text of each book. So, instead, we get *Bereshit* ("In the beginning ..."), *Shemot* ("Names"), *Vayikra* ("He called"), *Bamidbar* ("In the desert ...") and *Devarim* ("Words"). When these titles were translated into Greek by the writers of the Septuagint, the last book, *Devarim*, was translated "Deutero-nomos", meaning "second law". By doing so they translated the Hebrew word *Torah* as the Greek word *nomos*. And herein lies the problem. When they used the word *nomos* they got what they thought was the best fit. Every time they saw the word *Torah*, they translated it as *nomos*. This happened over 400 times. The trouble is that it wasn't always the perfect fit. *Nomos* is the suffix to a number of modern terms such as astronomy, economy and taxonomy and has the plain meaning of "law". In fact, *Nomos* was the Greek god of law, signifying the force of law, order and rationalism. It's not a subtle, textured word, it's a "what-you-see-on-the-label" type of word.

But *Torah* is different. We have already seen that its very essence comes from its root word of *yarah*, with the sense of being given the correct instructions or teaching to be able to shoot straight and hit the target. The abiding thought is of gentle coaxing, of God's hand resting on your shoulder and him saying, *go on my child, this is the way you should do it*. Contrast this with the harsh image of a fixed law, a command, a set of instructions that you must follow or else. That is *nomos*. Yet this is the mental image we have of *Torah*, of a set of laws rather than the love that is at the heart of them. A small child is punished for stepping into the road without looking but doesn't realise that it is his father's love behind that smack to the *tush*.

I've always puzzled at Psalm 119 and wondered why the psalmist would wax so lyrical about the Law. It makes no sense if the Law was seen as this restrictive and punishing set of rigid instructions. Yet we read:

> *I **rejoice** in following your statutes* ... (v. 14).
> *I **meditate** on your precepts* ... (v. 15).
> *I **delight** in your decrees* ... (v. 16).

I don't see many of us waxing so lyrical about a modern book of law! But the Jews at the time of the psalmist were conscious of the lawgiver rather than the "laws" themselves and knew that the purpose of the *Torah* was to give them instructions for life. There is a Hebrew word that encapsulates this idea:

הלכה *(hey – lamed – khaph – hey)* = *halachah*.

It refers to the practical outworking of these "instructions for life". The usual understanding and translation of this word is "Jewish Law", but its real and accurate translation is "the walk" or "the way to go".

Life is a journey, to coin a cliché, and the Hebraic mind sees obeying God's instructions as part of life, as part of our walk. After all, the very first Christians were known as the "people of the Way", people who lived according to these instructions. The emphasis is on the *doing* of God's Word, not just the *understanding* and discussing of the instructions, as we tend to do with our "Greek" upbringing. *Halachah* is not just about doing your religious duty, it is allowing God to guide you in all parts of your life, as that's what we've been created for. That's why, in the *Torah*, there were 613 instructions (*mitzvoth*), covering absolutely every aspect of life for the people of Israel as they meandered around in the desert.

The consequence of the English translators taking the word *nomos* and translating it as "law" in every case, is to give the impression that the Hebrew Scriptures, the "Old Testament" were all about the law, particularly in the sense of *legalistic regulations that are not in force any more*. This is contrasted with the New Testament, which is seen as being all about grace and therefore superseding the "Old Testament".

This is very black and white and is not just a characteristic of "Greek" thinking but very much the rearing of the head of an ancient, discredited heresy, *Marcionism*, which chose to create a division between the "Old" and the "New", even to the extent of diminishing the Jews and "their" God and exalting the Christians and "their" God. This is all very subtle but has survived the centuries and has driven a wedge between the "Old" and the "New" and between *law* and *grace*. These two, law and grace, or rather *teachings and grace*, are both a feature of God's interactions with mankind, whether in the Hebrew Scriptures of the Jews, the New Testament of the Christians, or in subsequent times. The grace that abounds to us as New Testament believers in the Lord Jesus Christ is nothing unless it is undergirded by his teachings, his instructions for life.

But, before we move on though, we mustn't allow those comments about Marcionism to deflect us from the very important truth that there is a central core within *Torah* that deals with our wicked nature and the necessary punishment for our sins. Otherwise, what is the need for the atoning death of Jesus?

> *Consider therefore the kindness and sternness of God: sternness to those who fell, but kindness to you, provided that you continue in his kindness. Otherwise, you also will be cut off* (Romans 11:22, NIV).

Perhaps the psalmist (Psalm 119:14–16) rejoiced and delighted in the law because it tells us how we can avoid God's wrath and punishment for unacceptable behaviour? He is just very thankful that God never sugar coats his words but tells us how it really is!

There is a group of people known as the *King James Only movement*. They are adamant that the King James Version (KJV) and that *alone* is the only acceptable English translation. [Note: It is also known as the Authorised Version (AV) meaning it was approved by King James I of England as the only Bible the Church of England would be authorised by Parliament to use (for some time).]

Others would take it even further. They would suggest that the *KJV* was actually divinely inspired, that the translators were given the same level of inspiration as the original writers, such as Moses and Ezra. Others would take it further still. They would suggest that the *KJV* was even more inspired than the original Hebrew version and should be the benchmark by which all other Hebrew Scripture should be evaluated, despite the fact that it was only an English translation. What do we make of this? Do these people have a case? Of course they don't! It's a translation, not canonical Scripture! And as for its alleged infallibility (if it's inspired surely it would have to be infallible), I think a case has been made that, for the "Old Testament", God chose Hebrew for a purpose. *God's signature* could not have been in any other language.

There are other reasons why we must declare that, rather than being an *inspired* translation of the "Old Testament", the KJV has fallibilities, due to being the fruits of the labours of mortal men. There are acknowledged translation errors, as well as many Hebrew idioms that are misunderstood and incorrectly translated, to say nothing of the archaic English words used, that may have gone down a hoot in 17th century taverns but would barely coax a raised eyebrow of acknowledgement in the *Dog and Duck* today. It's hard enough expecting modern English to fully express God's Word, but to impose an added level of confusion through the use of 'thee' and 'thou' is not the way forward.

───────────

However good a translation into English, or to any other language, there's always going to be something missing, and this is because God chose Hebrew as his language of revelation for a good reason. There's just something very special about the language. It may lack the sophistication and nuances of the European languages, but Merrill C. Tenney has rightly noted that Hebrew is able to incorporate much meaning in a few syllables, and that its dynamism can stir the reader profoundly, so it is suited to proclaiming God's words to mankind. (See *The Zondervan Pictorial Encyclopaedia*, p. 76.)

It truly encapsulates the Hebraic mindset, as distinct from the modern, "Greek" mindset. As I summarised in my book *To Life*:

> *Here's the problem. This Greek mindset, encouraging us to rely on brainpower to think everything through, is totally unsuitable for discerning the ways of God. And since the goal of every Christian is to discern God's ways for his/her life, we have ended up with an imbalance.*
>
> *God's revelation to us, his Holy Scripture, was written on his behalf by people who operated in the Hebraic mindset, a way of thinking that put God at the centre. And, just as you wouldn't use a Spanish dictionary to translate from Italian into English, the Greek mindset isn't the best tool to use to feed one's soul with God's instructions. So here we are, a folk who have learned to think in a certain logical, deductive, Greek way since our schooldays, encountering a Book that will only fully reveal its secrets to those who are trained to read it.* (pp. 80–81)

So, specifically, how is Hebrew uniquely qualified to reveal God's ways? We have already looked at this and we saw that one interesting feature is that it is *action-orientated*: it's good at explaining things, it's good at getting things done and it's happier with *verbs* than with nouns. In other words, as the Bible has been written to show us what we should *do* (i.e. our conduct) not only what we should *think*, then Hebrew must have been chosen for that reason. What about an example? Well, let's think of verbs.

A Hebrew verb is just bursting with information. We can look at it and discern the number, gender and identity of the person doing the action, as well as the cause of the action and the kind of action. The *cause* of the action is unique and not present in English and serves to tell us the motive of an action, a very useful feature to describe interactions between human beings and their God. This is called the *hiphil* form of the verb and here's an example.

Here's the Hebrew word for "he remembered":

זכר (zayin – khaph – resh)

And here's the *hiphil* form of the verb, with the meaning of "he reminded" (i.e. he *caused* to remember):

הזכר (hey – zayin – khaph – resh)

So we have to bear this all in mind when we consider translating from Hebrew into English. It's not just the agenda of the translator that we must consider, but the inadequacies of European languages to deal with the full meanings behind the Hebrew in God's Word. But English is our language, so we just have to deal with it.

There's a statue in a small church in Rome. It's Moses, as depicted by Michelangelo in the 16th century. There's one feature of this statue that is the result of a gross mistranslation of Hebrew Scripture: Moses has *two horns* on his head! It goes like this....

When Jerome translated the Hebrew Scriptures into Latin for the Catholic Church in the 4th century AD, he made the odd mistake. This was a *really* odd one. Here is Exodus 34:29 from the NIV:

> *When Moses came down from Mount Sinai with the two tablets of the Testimony in his hands, he was not aware that his face was radiant because he had spoken with the* Lord.
>
> [NIV]

This is basically what it said in the Masoretic text, but not in Jerome's translation, as turned into English by the *Douay-Rheims Bible*, a 16th century Bible prepared for the Catholic Church. This was how it translates that verse:

> *And when Moses came down from the mount Sinai, he held the two tables of the testimony, and he knew not that his face was **horned** from the conversation of the Lord.*

The difference is in bold, though you probably found it yourself. A straightforward mistranslation which did little to help the cause for Jewish-Christian relations when anti-Semitism was running wild in Europe!

There's not enough space here to go through the plethora of English translations that have popped up over the past few decades, but I will highlight a few of the major players.

The New International Version (NIV), first printed in 1978, is apparently the biggest selling Bible in the world, so it's worth looking at. It was very much produced as a joint effort. In their own words they state, '*... as a committee, we use what Bible translators call an "eclectic text" drawing on all the major published original texts, but making our own decisions about the textual variants found in those traditions.*' They also admit that, although they take the Masoretic text as their starting point, they make use of every other credible source available, including the *Masorah* notes in the margins of the Masoretic text.

There's a telling phrase in the Preface that states, "*... readings from these versions were occasionally followed where the Masoretic text seemed doubtful and where accepted principles of textual criticism showed that one or more of these textual witnesses **appeared** to provide the correct reading*". [My emphasis.]

Again we have human editorial control, and although sometimes this is vital for our understanding, there can be plenty of scope for bias, agenda, theological bent and prejudice to rear their heads. The key word in their phrase above is italicised: *appeared*. It's a word that alludes to human reason; it's a word that implies a decision made by a human being (or a committee of them) to decide what God is saying. Sometimes the cleverest of human minds can get it so wrong.

Does the fact that the NIV is the world's biggest selling Bible mean that it's God's chosen instrument or is it just a triumph of marketing? Between 1992 and 1997 the various ranges of NIV Bibles sold in quantities of between 750,000 and 6 million copies. In 2003 the publisher's marketing budget was said to be a six figure one, a lot of this going to the staggered launch of the "gender-neutral" *Today's New International Version* (TNIV). Its total market share that year was estimated to be around 45% of all Bibles sold in the USA.

Bibles have become big business and there are real profits to be made! In the case of a number of Bible publishing companies, ultimate ownership is in the hands of secular, profit-making corporations. I repeat, there's big bucks in the Holy Book. I wonder what the Lord thinks of this? Or could he be just happy that, profits aside, at least a worldwide marketing machine has been employed in propagating his Word? Do the ends justify the means in the economy of God?

However, the NIV certainly reads well, it's an effortless read, but can we have full confidence in what we are reading? What it boils down to is whether we have confidence in that particular team of translators who crafted the words. It's the same question we need to ask whatever Bible we are reading. Each has its own distinctive characteristics, its own strengths and its own failings. It's good to know such things.

In the UK, the NIV is marketed by Hodder Faith, who assure us in their current brochure that the 2011 revised edition has taken into account not just new biblical scholarship (good) and changes in the way we use language today (mmmm?), but also gender accurate language (*oy gevalt!*)

There is also a sports-themed Bible for the Olympics (that fortnight of celebration of nationalism and commercialism, with sport thrown in to give context) and a single-columned Bible in diary format. There are youth and children's Bibles, anglicised Bibles, even a *Thinline Lime soft-tone Bible*, perhaps for models to read on the catwalk?

So much pandering, so much dressing-up, every ounce of creative marketing effort to squeeze as much of 21st century culture into God's Word – no less than the Bible as fashion item, to be bought for others, but possibly, to be displayed rather than read, like that antique crockery on your mantelpiece, just gathering dust.

The Bible Society in the UK have just published two customised versions of the Common English Version (CEB) of the Bible. These are the *Freedom Bible*, with a sky blue cover and all verses on the subject of "Freedom" highlighted in sky blue and the *Poverty and Justice Bible*, likewise but in orangey-brown. Again, marketing campaigns have accompanied this endeavour and one wonders why. Why market Bible versions on a single theme, particularly themes that are not central themes of God's Word, but very much themes popular in today's world.

And that's the point. These are *focus group* Bibles, the products of market research and seemingly driven very much by the bottom line. These don't seem to be Bibles produced by the promptings of the Holy Spirit, filling a gap that other Bibles haven't reached. These may be filling a market gap, but it's to plug into the world's agenda, not God's. But then, I may be wrong and, of course, one mustn't dismiss the fact that God will use everything to reach the hearts of the lost, even a worldly-themed contextual translation of his words!

Another popular translation was the *Good News Bible* (GNB), published in 1966 as an easy-to-read version, good for children and non-native English speakers. Eugene Nida, the man in charge of the project at the American Bible Society, coined an expression, *dynamic equivalence*, to explain the philosophy behind the translation. This broke with every existing tradition and would have been anathema to those *Sopherim* and *Masoretes*, who treasured every Hebrew word, as if it were a living being. "Dynamic equivalence" looked at phrases, or thoughts, rather than individual words, and expressed the gist of each Bible passage as close as one could get to the original meaning. This undoubtedly made the translation easy to read, though accuracy in places has been sacrificed.

The "Old Testament" was translated by a committee of seven scholars and took nine years. They would have followed the same methodology as followed by the NIV translators, with heavy reliance on the Masoretic text, with other sources used as back-up.

So what about *dynamic equivalence* itself? Those who have translated the Scriptures that way – and there are a lot of them – are not so interested in the Hebrew words themselves, but rather what they feel lies *behind* the words; it is *thoughts*, rather than words, which interest them, and so this method opens up many possibilities ... for error. After all, words are plain to see, but God's thoughts...?

Here's what they would do, say, when translating the *Torah*, particularly the laws and regulations in, say, Leviticus. They would ask, *How would we (21st century English-speaking Christians) have responded if we had been around when Moses wrote that?* They would consider this for every event and proclamation by Moses, and then translate accordingly. Putting it another way, they would also say, *Let's pretend Moses was writing to us today. How would he have got his message across to us in our contemporary society?* Again, they would translate accordingly. Now we must ask ourselves: Was that God's intention? And, if not, what right have we to impose our own ideas and methodologies just to suit our current modern mindset?

Dynamic equivalence is a significant step away from what is unique and special about the Bible and towards man's world. Most modern translations are following this trend, pandering to the "needs" for clarity, acceptance and special interests (identified by marketing campaigns) rather than theological necessities. Even the publishers of the NIV have branched out and created more *relevant* translations for today's society, such as the TNIV, which is in more up-to-date English and veers towards a dynamic equivalence approach. It is also *gender-neutral*, pandering to the politically correct spirit of our age. As an example, Genesis 1:27 has been changed to "*So God created **human beings** in his own image*". [My emphasis.]

The warning in the Book of James seems apt here:

You adulterous people, don't you know that friendship with the world is hatred toward God? Anyone who chooses to be a friend of the world becomes an enemy of God (James 4:4, NIV and TNIV).

Then there's the *Revised Standard Version* (RSV) of the Bible. Chronologically, I suppose it would be the first of the modern translations, published in the 1950s as a serious challenge to the popularity of the King James Version and the first to include scholarship as a result of the Dead Sea Scrolls. It was not without its controversies, a major one going under the self-descriptive title of the "Isaiah 7:14 dispute". Seemingly pandering to Orthodox Jews, the RSV decided to offer this translation of the said verse:

Therefore the LORD himself will give you a sign. Behold, a young woman shall conceive and bear a son, and shall call his name Imman'u-el.

Can you see the source of the controversy? You will when I now offer the NIV translation of the same verse:

Therefore the Lord himself will give you a sign: The virgin will conceive and give birth to a son, and will call him Immanuel.

Yes, it's the *virgin* thing. Despite every other main Christian translation translating the Hebrew word *almah* as "virgin", the RSV, along with – as expected – the Jewish translations, translates it as "young woman" and therefore renders harmless a whole swathe of Christmas carols, as well as lessening a key theological element of the birth of our Messiah. Interestingly, the Catholic edition of the RSV in 2006, had "virgin" as the translation.

This wasn't the only controversy and they all seemed to be focused on Hebrew Scripture prophecies of the Messiah, a key one being in Daniel 9:25. Again can you spot the difference, a subtle one this time?

> *Know therefore and understand that from the going forth*
> *of the word to restore and build Jerusalem to the coming of*
> *an anointed one, a prince, there shall be seven weeks. Then*
> *for sixty-two weeks it shall be built again with squares and*
> *moat, but in a troubled time.* (RSV)

> *Know and understand this: From the time the word goes*
> *out to restore and rebuild Jerusalem until the Anointed One,*
> *the ruler, comes, there will be seven 'sevens,' and sixty-two*
> *'sevens.' It will be rebuilt with streets and a trench, but in*
> *times of trouble. (NIV)*

To many Christians, this is a powerful prophecy, providing an accurate prediction of when the Messiah was to come ... the first time. It is Daniel's "69 weeks" prophecy, for which there is no time here to expand (although there's a more detailed treatment in my book, *Jesus, Man of Many Names*) which is rendered meaningless in both the RSV and the Jewish translations, as the punctuation has this as Daniel's "7 weeks" prophecy instead, seeming to identify King Hezekiah as the "anointed one" of the text.

The RSV has had many critics. At the time, some Christians in the USA called it the "Red Bible", claiming it was communist-inspired, and one pastor even famously burned a copy in the pulpit, sending the ashes to the head of the translating committee. You can admire their zeal, but perhaps not their deductions and actions!

Probably the most famous and widely used *paraphrase* translation of the Bible is *The Message* by Eugene Peterson. It takes *dynamic equivalence* to its extreme and is basically God's Word interpreted through the eyes of a Christian novelist, written in a modern style and conveying the *gist* of the Hebrew Scriptures, without the power that can only come in its fullest sense through the words themselves (even when translated into another language). It is, in a sense, the Bible as a *jolly good read* and although there is value in using it to introduce the Bible to the masses, one would hope *the masses* are encouraged to progress to a more literal translation of God's Word at the earliest opportunity!

You'll enjoy the stories but you won't necessarily meet the Author on his terms (though he has a way of breaking through despite the "restrictions" we place on him!)

We must now pause, take breath, then remind ourselves what the Bible *is*. It is God's Word to mankind (or should I say *humankind*!?) It is not primarily a series of nice stories, morality tales, character studies, history, poetry or warnings. There is a framework (just as our skeleton, organs and fleshy bits provide our framework for life) which includes narrative, history, ethics, poetry, prophecy, promise, fulfilment, and much more of course. The key point is that the Bible is alive with the breath of God; we meet with him through the study of his Word, and want to be as close to his original meanings as we can get.

It started with God's finger on the mountain, then his dictation of the *Torah* to Moses, who faithfully reproduced these divine instructions on scrolls, which were stored, neglected, then found and used to instigate a religious revival, first under King Josiah, then later with Ezra the *Sopher*. The same man, along with associates, then began to draw together other divinely inspired writings, from prophets, historians, poets and soldiers, creating the collection of holy writings, the Holy Scriptures. A copy was kept in the Jerusalem Temple but generations of *Sopherim* faithfully created accurate copies, handing over the responsibility eventually to the *Masoretes*, who produced the definitive Hebrew Scriptures, used now in its entirety in Jewish Bibles and forming the basis of the Christian "Old Testament" in the various Bibles now available to us today.

Surely, if we want a relationship with God then we need to form a working relationship with his Word, the Scriptures. If I want to get into the head of Tolstoy I read *War and Peace*, I don't watch the BBC TV serial, starring Anthony Hopkins. If I wish to understand C.S. Lewis and what drives him, I read the book, I don't watch the cartoon. Or perhaps I am simply demonstrating my personal preferences here.

The "Old Testament", the *Tenach*, the Hebrew Scriptures – they are God's Word to us and it's time to take them seriously.

Part Two

The Journey within God's Word

Chapter Twelve

Of Man

We begin this section with a short selection of Hebrew word studies based on ourselves, our creation, identity, shortcomings, and our relationship with our Creator. We start with an intriguing mystery.

It's in the second chapter of Genesis. It's regarding this verse, concerning the creation of man:

> The LORD God **formed** the man from the dust of the ground and breathed into his nostrils the breath of life, and the man became a living being (Genesis 2:7). [My emphasis, here as elsewhere.]

To be more exact, it's regarding the Hebrew of this verse, or to be even more focused, the Hebrew word translated as *formed*. The word is:

וייצר *(vav – yod – yod – tsade – resh)* = *vayitzer.*

Now let's compare it with a similar verse later on in the chapter, concerning the creation of the animals:

> Now the LORD God had **formed** out of the ground all the beasts of the field and all the birds of the air (Genesis 2:19).

In this case, the Hebrew word translated as *formed* is this:

וייצר *(vav – yod – tsade – resh)* = *vayitzer.*

It's pronounced the same as the one in verse 7, but there's one difference. Have you spotted it? In the creation of man the word has *two* yods (״), but in the creation of the animals there's only *one* yod (׳). So, what do we say to this? I said earlier that the *Masoretes* and the *Sopherim* weren't infallible – so *it's probably just a spelling mistake?* Yes? No! God *is* infallible and these verses are too foundational for God to allow an error like this to creep in. Also, it's too glaring an error to be missed by generations of *Sopherim* – someone would have noticed it and done something about it. No doubt they *did* notice it – and left it in, for good reason.

So what is God saying here? In the *Talmud* (*Tractate Berakoth* 61a), Rabbi Nahman suggests that the two *yods* are two inclinations of man, the good inclination and the evil one (just like those comedies where the miniature devil and angel are sitting on each shoulder, whispering advice into the ear). But then the *Talmud* puzzles over why, if animals only have one inclination (presumably the good one), they still injure, bite and kick!

Others, including many influential rabbis such as Rashi, have suggested that the extra *yod* in mankind's creation is because we have a soul and animals don't have a soul. This is further explained by the fact that, in some places in the Hebrew Scriptures, the *double yod* is used as an abbreviation of God's sacred name.

״

This gives the picture of God living through us, as an extra spiritual input into our lives, through his Spirit into our *soul*. It's quite a comforting thought, to see it *literally* spelled out!

There are two profound thought processes going on in these types of word studies. Firstly that God expects us to question things. He is glad when we notice things like this *double yod*. There doesn't have to be a definite answer, as the feature of the Hebraic mindset is the continuous discussion, debate and arguing. And, of course, any answer we may come up with *must* be consistent with God's character as revealed in Scripture. There doesn't always have to be a definite answer, *but there always must be a question.* To question God's Word is to engage with it, to caress it, to love it, to treat it as a living being, not a dead remnant from ancient history.

That's my first thought. My second is the consequence of our *double yod.* Whatever the truth may be, the fact remains that there was something *different* in the creation of man and beast. We are different from the animals – we didn't evolve from one! This addition of a *yod,* the smallest letter in the Hebrew alphabet, should put paid to any doubts that we are a *special creation.* God has shown this in his Word, but we had to dig deep into the Hebrew to find it. Now you can see how exciting these studies can be!

Now we return to the first verse that we have already examined:

> *The LORD God formed the **man** from the dust of the **ground** and breathed into his nostrils the breath of life, and the man became a living being* (Genesis 2:7).

We are going to look at it again, but from a different angle, looking at the two words in bold, *man* and *ground.* Here are the two words:

אדם *(aleph – dalet – Mem)* = *adam* = *man.*

אדמה *(aleph – dalet – mem – hey)* = *adamah* = *ground.*

It's hard to miss the connection. *The LORD God formed the **adam** from the dust of the **adamah**.* It's a bit of Hebrew wordplay here, grounding man in the ... ground. Seems straightforward, but then we see a similar wordplay a little bit further along, in the story of Cain and Abel, when God confronts the guilty brother:

> *The LORD said, "What have you done? Listen! Your brother's **blood** cries out to me from the **ground**"* (Genesis 4:10).

Here are the two words:

דם *(dalet – Mem)* = **dam** = *blood.*

אדמה *(aleph – dalet – mem – hey)* = **adamah** = *ground.*

Again there's a connection and we now have three words – man, ground and blood – all sharing the same root and all connected. Blood is what sustains man and we are aware of the verse in Leviticus:

For the life of a creature is in the blood (Leviticus 17:11).

It's all very grounding, and it's worth noticing that the word *adam* (אדם) is the word for *blood* (דם) preceded by the letter *aleph* (א). This letter, as we have seen before, signifies leadership, strength or headship. So a man is someone who is *in control of his blood*, rather than controlled by it, as with the animal kingdom. Another way of looking at this – and there are always lots of ways of looking at things in the Hebraic mindset – is that Adam is the *first blood*, the first of the bloodline of the human race.

――――――

Sometimes in Scripture we see a slight variation in the word *Adam.*

האדם *(hey – aleph – dalet – Mem)* = **ha-adam** = *man or mankind*

The *ha* (ה) prefix broadens the meaning to *mankind*, depending on context. One such place is this:

I gave them my decrees and made known to them my laws, for the man who obeys them will live by them (Ezekiel 20:11).

The sense that we get here (in all the English translations) is that the only people who must live by the decrees are those who were

in the Mosaic covenant [the covenant given through Moses] (i.e.
Israel). It conveys the impression that this verse is just for the
Hebrews, who were living under that covenant. But the intention, shown by the use of הָאָדָם, is a lot broader. It is for *all*
mankind, not just the Jews. This prompts an interesting question: *How can this be for everyone if the decrees of the Torah
were meant just for the Jews?* Are those Gentiles who have been
grafted in under the new covenant (see Jeremiah 31:31; Romans
11:17) included here? Are believers in *Yeshua* (Gentiles mainly,
but also some Jews) meant to be keeping *any* of the *Torah*? What
an interesting topic for discussion. Don't expect to get any pat
answers here, but read Galatians, Hebrews and Romans chapter
1, and pray that the Lord gives you wisdom in such matters. And
you could look out for my next book!

That's enough about Adam; we now turn our thoughts to the
almighty mess he left us in, our inherited sinful nature. Did you
know that Hebrew has twenty-four words for *sin*? It can be
argued that English has the same, but in our case it's because
we're frightened of the word and wish to dilute its meaning. We
use such words as peccadillo, mistake, disobedience, misdeed,
wrongdoing, not because the word "sin" is hard to understand,
rather that it's hard for us to accept it. Not so with Hebrew,
which is not afraid to confront the truth, but which really has
twenty-four different ways of looking at it. So when you see the
word "sin" in the Bible you must ask *which of the twenty-four
meanings am I to take here?* Here is such a case:

> *Surely I was sinful at birth, sinful from the time my mother
> conceived me* (Psalm 51:5).

Even the two words used here are from different Hebrew
words.

עָוֹן *(ayin – vav – Nun)* = **avon** = *sin, iniquity.*

חטא *(chet – tav – aleph)* = **chattah** = *sin.*

This second word means sin, offence or a fault, *actions that lead to a punishment.* But look at the context here, does this mean that the newborn has violated the *Torah* in some way and is deserving of punishment? What about the ovum and sperm at the moment of conception? What on earth did they do that was wrong? Does original sin have consequences for foetuses and babies? What did David mean when he penned this psalm?

When we look at the word חטא (*chattah*), the root word, חט, in its ancient meaning, conveyed the idea of separation or being cut off from the covenant or community. It took the meaning that if you sinned against anyone in the community, then you should be cut off from the community. In Hebrew thought, the deed itself carried with it the consequence, so the Hebrew word for "sin" here also implied the punishment for the sin, which is separation from the community and from God.

David was a man acutely conscious of his sins, something clearly borne out by this psalm. *Chattah* was a word used in the Psalms nearly always in cries of woe and anguish. And it was all about community. The Hebraic mindset is more about community than individuals and these cries of woe reflect David's pain at hurting his community, his family, even to the extent that such sins can travel along generational lines, affecting those who come after us. So, when David pondered, he was reminding himself also of his ancestors' sins, not necessarily blaming them for all that had gone wrong in his own life, but acknowledging how bound up we all are in our families, for good or bad.

The English word "sin" really doesn't paint much of a picture, does it? Perhaps we should invent twenty-four English words, relating to each Hebrew word, so that we can understand the subtleties behind the word.

Finally, our thoughts turn from inwards to outwards, from contemplating our navels to marvelling at our Father in heaven. How do we see our God? Do we *delight* in him? This Psalm tells us:

> *Delight yourself in the LORD and he will give you the desires of your heart* (Psalm 37:4).

Perhaps the Hebrew is telling us more? Let's look at the key word.

עַנָּג *(ayin – nun – gimmel)* = *'anag* = delight

This word's basic meaning is to be soft, delicate or dainty with something. Surely this is all a bit "girly", isn't it? What it is really saying is that we should delight in God as we would delight in, say, a piece of silk. We should marvel in the object alone just for what it is. In the same way we should delight in God just for who he is, not for what he has done for us. Our "Greek" thinking tends to be very utilitarian – *you do something for me then I'll do something for you* – but Hebraic understanding is to marvel at our great God just for who he is. This is reinforced when we look at the Canaanite word pictures for the letters of this word:

⌐ ˥ ⊖

The basic meaning is to see life lifted up and, as God *is* our life, then we should lift him up. Other uses of this word are in Deuteronomy 28:56, where it is used to express delicacy, and in Isaiah 66:11, to show the delight of Jerusalem being restored. We should be delighted in the Lord in the way that Jesus describes it thus:

> *"The kingdom of heaven is like treasure hidden in a field. When a man found it, he hid it again, and then in his joy went and sold all he had and bought that field"* (Matthew 13:44).

So, given that we *delight* in the LORD, what should our response be? Let's first look at the response of the Hebrews, when Moses had given them God's offer to be his people:

> *"Now if you obey me fully and keep my covenant, then out of all nations you will be my treasured possession. Although the whole earth is mine"* (Exodus 19:5).

Actually this is the closest you're going to get to God SHOUT-ING at his people. Let's look at that phrase, "obey me fully".

שמוע תשמעוּ *(shin – mem – vav – ayin tav – shin – mem – ayin – vav)* = *shamoa tishmeoo*

Look at the Hebrew words. They share a root:

שמע *(shin – mem – ayin)* = *shama'* = hear, obey

What God is saying is *hear – OBEY!* He is emphasising his command to them. Hear me! Obey me! He's speaking through a loud-hailer! He is trying to show the Hebrews exactly how important this is going to be to them, because there are going to be terrible penalties for disobedience. So what *was* their response?

> *The people all responded together, "We will do everything the LORD has said." So Moses brought their answer back to the LORD* (Exodus 19:8).

Unfortunately ... well you know the rest! They heard, but did they obey? Did they really do everything the Lord had said? Biblical history from that point onwards is basically a commentary on the disobedience of God's people.

Chapter Thirteen
Of Messiah

Now we all know that "Jesus" isn't his real name, don't we? Despite what it says in Matthew 1:21:

> *"She will give birth to a son, and you are to give him the name Jesus, because he will save his people from their sins."*

There's nothing intrinsically special about the English name *Jesus* that conjures up the concept of "saving people from their sins". So perhaps it's his Greek name that Matthew is referring to as, after all, the New Testament was written in Greek. The Greek name is *Iesous*, which also wasn't his real name, as he wasn't Greek. Jesus was Jewish, so we have to use his real *Hebrew* name which was this:

ישוע *(yod – shin – vav – ayin)* = *yeshua*.

This means, "The Lord saves." Now Matthew 1:21 makes sense:

> *"She will give birth to a son, and you are to give him the name Jesus, **because he will save his people from their sins.**"*

But we can take this even further when we look deeper into his name. It is derived from the following 3-letter root, meaning *to save* or *salvation*. You can see how the vowels can make a subtle difference, as the consonants are identical!

ישׁע *(yod – shin – ayin)* = *yasha* = *to save.*
ישׁעי *(yod – shin – ayin)* = *yesha* = *salvation.*

The second example appears in a strategic place in Isaiah 61:10:

I delight greatly in the LORD;
my soul rejoices in my God.
For he has clothed me with garments of **salvation**
and arrayed me in a robe of righteousness,
as a bridegroom adorns his head like a priest,
and as a bride adorns herself with her jewels.

The preceding verses in Isaiah 61 constitute the C.V. for the coming Messiah, verses that Jesus himself quoted in Luke chapter 4, speaking of himself.

"The Spirit of the LORD *is on me, because he has anointed me to preach good news to the poor. He has sent me to proclaim freedom for the prisoners and recovery of sight for the blind, to release the oppressed, to proclaim the year of the* LORD's *favour"* (vv. 18–19).

So it's interesting to see *Yeshua* (Jesus) implicated in that highly prophetic passage in Isaiah, clearly speaking about himself. How apt his name was going to be.

We also read in Exodus:

Moses answered the people, "Do not be afraid. Stand firm and you will see the **deliverance** *the* LORD *will bring you today. The Egyptians you see today you will never see again."*

(14:13)

This is a key event in the life of the Jews. Moses is calming his people down. He is asking them to have faith in the deliverance to come, the parting of the Red Sea to save them from the Egyptians. Salvation will come to all who believe. It's a God thing, an

"Old Testament" thing as well as the central message of the New Testament. And here in Exodus 14:13 is where we see it first. And here is the key word used for this salvation:

ישׁוּעָת *(yod – shin – vav – ayin – tav)* = **yeshuat** = *deliverance (in NIV) /salvation (in Jewish Bible)*

Again, implicit within another key prophetic passage, such as this, is the coming of *Yeshua* (Jesus). This word, ישׁוּעָ, appears in 77 places throughout the Hebrew Scriptures. You can find them yourself if you have Strong's Hebrew Lexicon (number #3444). So the person of *Yeshua*/Jesus is implicated all over the "Old Testament", though we shouldn't necessarily get too carried away in every case, as the context is not always the same.

It is interesting that there's another loosely related word used of Jesus. It's not a surname but rather a title related to his kingship: *Christ*. Here is Peter's declaration:

Simon Peter answered, "You are the Christ, the Son of the living God." (Matthew 16:16)

Again, we reverse engineer the real name in Hebrew and we get this:

משׁיח *(mem – shin – yod – chet)* = **mashiach** = *messiah.*

This time the English word bears some sort of relation to the Hebrew one. If we look at other words that come from the same three-letter root, we'll start to see the *real* meaning of the word.

    mashach = to anoint, consecrate
    mashuach = oiled, anointed
    mishchah = ointment
    mashchah = consecrated portion

The Messiah, משׁיח, is the anointed one. We can see this word in the Hebrew Scriptures in a chapter we have already looked at, in Isaiah 61:

> "*The Spirit of the Sovereign* LORD *is on me, because the* LORD **has anointed me** *to preach good news to the poor. He has sent me to bind up the brokenhearted, to proclaim freedom for the captives and release from darkness for the prisoners*" (v. 1).

And it is repeated in Luke 4:

> "*The Spirit of the* LORD *is on me, because he* **has anointed me** *to preach good news to the poor. He has sent me to proclaim freedom for the prisoners and recovery of sight for the blind, to release the oppressed, to proclaim the year of the Lord's favour*" (vv. 18–19).

The Hebrew word used is:

משח *(mem – shin – chet)* = **mashach** = *anointed*.

So Jesus Christ is:

ישוע משיח Yeshua Mashiach = Jesus Messiah, or, to be more precise:

ישוע המשיח Yeshua HaMashiach = Jesus *the* Messiah = Jesus Christ.

Or, for his full descriptive name and title in English, *The* LORD *saves, the anointed one.*

Now I mentioned a little earlier that Jesus' name and title were loosely related. Well, if you look at both words above you'll see a common letter, ש , the *shin*. Very interesting letter.

ש

It has always been seen as a very holy letter, even from its very appearance. It evokes natural phenomena that burst upwards to the heavens, as a tree's branches reaching for the sky or a bed of flowers growing upwards, longing to receive sustenance from above. It also reminds us of the faith of Moses and you can see him (sort of), as the middle branch of the letter, the outside ones being his outstretched arms, as Israel prevailed in battle against the Amalekites.

> *As long as Moses held up his hands, the Israelites were winning, but whenever he lowered his hands, the Amalekites were winning* (Exodus 17:11).

The other visual features are the three prongs, the three units, evoking, in Jewish writings (*Midrash*) the spirit, soul and body *or* this world, the Messianic era and the world to come. To the Christian mind it evokes the Trinity, the three-in-one, God in three persons. To have a *shin* in each word is to remind us that God is in the midst of us, he is intimately involved in our salvation through *Yeshua*, the *anointed one*.

Of course, this may just be a fanciful notion but, as I said earlier, *there doesn't always have to be a definite answer, but there always must be a question*. If we look for God we will find him; the more that reminds us of him, the more we will think of him, the closer he will be to us. It's not always about whether we are wrong or right, it's often about the journey we take to get there. And every journey that has God as a destination also has him showing us the way....

———————

But the Messiah has other names too. We read of them in that awesome verse, Isaiah 9:6:

> *For to us a child is born, to us a son is given, and the government will be on his shoulders. And he will be called Wonderful Counsellor, Mighty God, Everlasting Father, Prince of Peace.*

This, of course, is referring to the Messiah, *Yeshua ben Yosef*
(Jesus, son of Joseph), yet it's full of other names for him. What's
this all about then?

Well there are four extra names for him here. They are not
names as we understand them but descriptive titles, which
Hebrew names tend to be. Let's look at each in turn.

פלא יועץ *(pey – lamed – aleph yod – vav – ayin – Tsade)*
= *pele yo'eyts* = wonderful counsellor.

The word **פלא** (wonderful) is only used 12 other times in Scripture and virtually every time it is used in reference to God alone.
The word **יעץ** (counsellor) has a deeper, more dynamite-charged
meaning than the English can convey. It's far more proactive, not
just counselling and advising but also executing and planning.
This child who is to be born won't just tell us what to do but will
set an example and show us what to do. That's Jesus down to a
tee! In fact his first followers are known by the familiar term of
disciple (*talmid* in Hebrew), who didn't just learn at his feet, but
were told to *do likewise*.

אל גבור *(aleph – lamed gimel – bet – vav – resh)*
= *el gibbor* = mighty God.

We've already met the generic name for God (**אל**). The other
word, **גבור** (gibbor), is an interesting one, a powerful one, not a
word used for women or children, yet here it is, used for a child!
This is a child born to do mighty deeds, not the ordinary stuff
that fills up our ordinary lifetimes, but terrible, powerful deeds,
to dwarf anything we are capable of.

אביעד *(aleph – bet – yod – ayin – Dalet)*
= *aviad* = eternal Father.

Now we've already met the word for "father", *avi* (**אב**), it's
a key little sliver of Hebrew, made up of the first two words of
the alphabet (*aleph – bet*). This new word, *aviad*, combines this

with the word for "eternal or continuing or perpetual", *ad* (עַד).
Together we get the picture of a God who we can trust forever,
and the special purpose of this word, used in this context, is all
tied up in family, God's family, this *child* to be born, who is also
our *father*.

שַׂר שָׁלוֹם *(sin – resh shin – lamed – vav – Samech)*
= *sar shalom* = Prince of Peace.

This is a familiar term to us Christians; it's a title we often use
for Jesus the Messiah. It is also a favoured title for many Messianic Christian fellowships worldwide. What do these words
evoke for you? Perhaps a gentle, bearded man stroking a dove, or
some similar imagery? The word *sar* (שַׂר) is often used for a sub-
ordinate character, perhaps a defeated king. This is *not* a word
that sits well in a passage following two powerful descriptions
of Almighty God. Yet it is used here and tells us that our mighty
God, everlasting Father, is also going to come to us in humility.
It's an amazing expression and must have been so confusing to
those of Isaiah's day, or even to rabbis who subsequently rejected
the Messiah, yet have to reconcile these two natures of the Messiah, without considering the one who *did* come as a Prince of
Peace, yet is still Mighty God.

It is intriguing that in many Jewish translations of this passage,
for instance many earlier JPS Hebrew Bibles, the full expression
was originally just *transliterated* – it was only translated into
English in later editions. So this is what you would have read:

... *and his name is called Pele-joez-el-gibbor-abi-ad-sar-
shalom....*

How strange. Could it have been that this Messianic title just
screamed out the "forbidden one", *Yeshua* and so was left
untranslated? It's worth a thought.

We return to that wonderful Messianic scripture, Isaiah 9:6, but
this time we focus on what seems to be an anomaly. *Surely not*,
I hear you shout. Read on. ...

We have already seen that there are five letters in the Hebrew alphabet that take on a different form when they are at the end of a word. One of them is the letter *mem*.

מ Here it is at the beginning of a word e.g. מָשִׁיחַ (mashiach).
ם And here it is at the end of a word e.g. שָׁלוֹם (shalom).

The מ is called an *open* mem because of the small opening on the bottom left, whereas ם is a closed mem because it is closed from all sides. Hebrew grammar insists that the closed mem *only* appears at the end of the word, which is the case ... **except in one place:**

> *For to us a child is born, to us a son is given, and the government will be on his shoulders. And he will be called Wonderful Counsellor, Mighty God, Everlasting Father, Prince of Peace.* **Of the increase** *of his government and peace there will be no end. He will reign on David's throne and over his kingdom, establishing and upholding it with justice and righteousness from that time on and forever. The zeal of the* LORD *Almighty will accomplish this* (Isaiah 9:6–7).

This is the famous Messianic declaration that we have recently looked at, declaring the titles of the coming Messiah. The anomaly is in bold, it's the Hebrew word translated "of the increase".

לְםַרְבֵּה *(lamed – mem – resh – bet – hey) = l'marbeh = of the increase.*

The *closed mem* is underlined above. Surely it should have been an *open* one?

Could this be a spelling mistake? After all, the *closed mem* is very similar to another letter, the *samech*, which is a tad more rounded. But again, as with the *double yods* in Genesis 2, this has appeared in a hugely significant piece of Scripture. It would have been spotted and corrected if it had been a mistake, but instead it has been allowed to remain. Why?

Firstly, how have the rabbis explained it? One view has been that the person being talked about here was Hezekiah, a later king of Judah who, through his actions in not praising God when the enemy army was destroyed, had the open mem *closed off*, only to be opened when the true Messiah comes. Interesting ... but unlikely. I suggested that God's Word was alive but not to the extent of letters altering their shapes willy-nilly!

Intriguingly, in the *Zohar*, Jewish mystical writings at the heart of *Kabbalah*, the view is that the *closed mem* indicates that the Messiah will be born from a *closed* womb. A closed womb? Isn't that a virgin birth? The Messiah coming from the closed womb of a virgin? What an idea! So the rabbis really did think of it first! As an added reminder, the letter *mem*, is the first letter of the name of the virgin who did give birth to the Messiah. Her name was Miriam (translated as Mary). Also, the Hebrew word for womb, is *me'em*, also beginning with a *mem*.

Are there other places in the Hebrew Scriptures where Hebrew letters themselves seem to be speaking of the coming Messiah? Of course there are. Here's one short study that takes us back almost to the beginning. Here are two verses:

> *This is the **account** of the heavens and the earth when they were created. When the* LORD *God made the earth and the heavens ...* (Genesis 2:4).

> *This is the **written account** of Adam's line. When God created man, he made him in the likeness of God* (Genesis 5:1).

The words in bold are in fact the same Hebrew word, but spelt in two different ways.

תוֹלְדוֹת *(tav – vav – lamed – dalet – vav – tav)* = *toledot* = *generations/account.*

The above is the spelling in Genesis 2:4. And below is the spelling of the word in Genesis 5:1 (and also in Genesis 6:9; 10:1; 10:32; 11:10; 11:27; 25:12–13; 25:19; 36:1; 36:9; 37:2 and 25 other places).

תולדת *(tav – vav – lamed – dalet – tav)* = *toledot* = *generations/account.*

You can see the difference. There is a missing *vav* in Genesis 5:1. So what? Scribal error? Spelling mistake? The rabbis didn't think so. They noticed that the correct spelling of the word, throughout Scripture, was with the *vav* missing and they asked why did the *vav* disappear after Genesis 2:4? There *had* to be a reason. God *must* have had a reason for this! Now every letter in the Hebrew alphabet has a number equivalent, from aleph (1) to tav (22), and they noticed that *vav* is the sixth letter of the alphabet and therefore has the numerical equivalent of six. Something happened to Adam after Genesis 2:4 – the Fall – when he lost *six things*. These were his glorious sheen (Job 14:20), life (Genesis 3:19), his stature (Genesis 3:8), the fruit of the ground (Genesis 3:17) and the heavenly lights (Genesis 1:14). Yes, there are only five in this list and it doesn't seem to make perfect sense to us, but one would have to get inside the mind of a rabbi to fully appreciate what is meant here. Mmm. A bit random, perhaps? But then they notice something else. They looked at Ruth 4:18:

*This, then, is the **family line** of Perez: Perez was the father of Hezron. ...*

And here's the Hebrew word for "family line":

תולדות *(tav – vav – lamed – dalet – vav – tav)* = *toledot* = *generations/account*

The *vav* has returned! The rabbis say (and we would agree) that in Ruth 4 we have the Messianic line, the list of forbears of the Messiah. Here's the rest of the Chapter:

> *Hezron the father of Ram, Ram the father of Amminadab, Amminadab the father of Nahshon, Nahshon the father of Salmon, Salmon the father of Boaz, Boaz the father of Obed, Obed the father of Jesse, and Jesse the father of David* (Ruth 4:19–22).

And it was said that the Messiah would *bring back those six things that were lost!* Thought-provoking and interesting, certainly.

There's another Scripture that speaks of this Messianic line, tracing it back to one of the sons of Jacob, one of the people of Israel:

> *The sceptre will not depart from Judah, nor the ruler's staff from between his feet, until he comes to whom it belongs and the obedience of the nations is his* (Genesis 49:10, NIV).

The King James Version is more familiar to us, with "until Shiloh come" rather than "until he comes" and referring to "gathering" rather than "nations". It's that word *Shiloh*. It looks like the NIV translators have translated it for us, giving us "he to whom it belongs". But is this the only interpretation? Here's the Hebrew word:

שילה *(shin – yod – lamed – hey)* = *shiloh* = ?

The English translation of the Jewish Bible has it slightly differently:

> *The staff shall not depart from Judah, nor the sceptre from between his feet, until peace come, and the obedience of the people be unto him.*

This translation is probably closer to the true meaning. We have to remember what we covered in Chapter 2 to find out why.

This is when we were looking at the 3-letter root system and in particular the root of this word:

שלם

This is the old Christian favourite Hebrew word *shalom*, giving the meaning of peace, completeness and wholeness. You can see how close this is to the root of *shiloh*, which is why the Jewish translators wrote what they did. So a better translation here would surely be in the style of the King James Version, which is consistent with both Jewish and Christian expectations *of a coming Messiah*. This Messiah will come from the line of Judah, he will be a lawgiver and he will give peace (*shalom*). But who is this Messiah for? If this was to be a Messiah solely for the Jews then the Hebrew should reflect this. But it doesn't. This is the word used for who this Messiah is for:

עמים *(ayin – mem – yod – Mem)* = *amim* = peoples.

The word used here, *amim*, is a plural word, meaning "peoples", in the sense of all peoples of the world. If this Messiah was to be for just Israel then the Hebrew word used would have been עם (am), meaning just a *single* people.

So Jesus is meant for all, even Gentiles! And this truth was declared as far back as the first book in the Bible.

For our last two studies we are going to look at the very character of the coming Messiah. Firstly, let us return to a recurring theme in this book – the use of Hebrew names. We have already discovered how Hebrew names are just bursting with meaning, giving perfect descriptions of either the character or the mission of the person in question. We are now going to look at one of the minor characters in the Hebrew Scriptures, a woman of substance. Here is her name first in the ancient Canaanite word pictures:

This literally means *a person who controls what separates,* someone in control of the fence that surrounds them. Have you guessed who we are referring to yet? Here is her name in Hebrew:

רחל *(resh – chet – lamed) = rachel.*

Rachel was Jacob's choice of wife, though he had to wait a bit before it all worked out for the two of them. It was through her son, Joseph, that God carried out his plans to save the people of Israel from the famine, and her name resounds through the centuries as "Rachel weeping for her children", a sad declaration from Jeremiah and Matthew, with poignant applications during the horrors of the Holocaust.

Back to the word pictures and to the idea of someone in control of her surroundings. The letter *chet* used here is also used in the sense of privacy, so a better meaning could be a woman in control of her private life. This is a *woman of purity.* When we look at the Hebrew dictionary definition of Rachel, the chief meaning is of a *ewe,* a female lamb, but it also conveys the idea of being delicate, innocent and sensitive, giving the idea of one with innocence and purity. These days, the word "Rachel" is associated with the expression "as innocent as a lamb". There's also a mention of this word in Isaiah 53:7:

> *He was oppressed and afflicted, yet he did not open his mouth; he was led like a lamb to the slaughter, and* **as a sheep before her shearers** *is silent, so he did not open his mouth.*

Here's a part of that verse in Hebrew:

וברחל לפני like a Rachel (ewe) before her shearers.

Let's think of the imagery here. Unlike the male sheep (ram), the ewe does not resist the shearer. Rachel is submitting voluntarily; she does not allow her purity to be violated. Here we can see a connection with Jesus that is often overlooked because the

English translations cannot convey the levels of meaning of the
original Hebrew.

We finish this chapter with a flourish, with a glimpse into
the world of typology – how something in the Hebrew
Scriptures can speak in many interesting ways of the Messiah to
come.

The tabernacle in the desert. There's a lot we can learn there,
but we are just going to follow a few threads and see where
they take us. These "threads" just happen to be in the curtain
that separated the *Holy Place* from the *Most Holy Place* in the
tabernacle.

> *Make a curtain of blue, purple and scarlet yarn and finely*
> *twisted linen, with cherubim worked into it by a skilled*
> *craftsman* (Exodus 26:31).

The first thing that the Hebrew tells us is that there are four colours indicated here, not just blue, purple and scarlet. We look at
the Hebrew word for linen:

שׁשׁ *(shin – shin)* = **shesh** = linen.

It also has the meaning of *something bleached white*, the colour of purity and righteousness, a natural barrier between God
and man, because of our natural unrighteousness. OK, but what
of the other three colours, what is the symbolism there?

First the purple. Here is the Hebrew word:

ארגמן *(aleph – resh – gimmel – mem – Nun)* = **argaman** =
purple.

This word specifically refers to a fiery reddish purple, a dye
so expensive it could only be obtained through single droplets
from the throat of a particular shellfish. It is the royal colour,
the colour of kings, supposedly reflected by the very *shekinah*

glory of God and the colour most connected to the promised Messiah-King.

Now the scarlet. Here are the words used in the verse:

וְתוֹלַעַת שָׁנִי *(vav – tav – vav – lamed – ayin – tav shin – nun – yod) = **tolaat shani** = scarlet worm.*

Scarlet is the colour of blood, speaking of the *atonement*. And it all comes from a despised worm, reminiscent of that great messianic Psalm 22:6, which uses the same word, speaking of the one whose blood was going to atone for our sins.

> *But I am a worm and not a man, scorned by men and despised by the people.*

And of courses *scarlet*, in terms of the atonement, is used in this key verse:

> *"Come now, let us reason together," says the* LORD. *"Though your sins are like **scarlet**, they shall be as white as snow"* (Isaiah 1:18).

Finally, the blue colour. In a way this is an obvious one (though perhaps not so much in the UK) as it represented the blue skies over the land. There are two associated traditions here, firstly that the Ark inside the Tabernacle was covered with a blue cloth when transported, and secondly, that the Messiah will come out of the blue sky above. Pointing to the Temple and acknowledging the high priest, Zechariah speaks thus:

> *"Tell him this is what the* LORD *Almighty says: 'Here is the **man** whose name is the Branch, and he will branch out from his place and build the temple of the* LORD*"* (Zechariah 6:12).

This word, *branch*, is an interesting one.

צמח *(tsade – mem – chet)* = ***tsemach*** = sprout, branch, shoot.

It also appears in the following verses:

> *"The days are coming," declares the* LORD, *"when I will raise up to David a righteous Branch, a **King** who will reign wisely and do what is just and right in the land"* (Jeremiah 23:5).

> *"Listen, O high priest Joshua and your associates seated before you, who are men symbolic of things to come: I am going to bring my **servant**, the Branch"* (Zechariah 3:8).

So this *branch* is a man, a King and a Servant (all highlighted above). Nothing other than the Messiah, the King-Redeemer-Man, represented by this *branch*, but also by that curtain in the Tabernacle, as the bridge between man and God, represented by the colours purple (King), scarlet (Redeemer) and blue (Messiah). And *that's* our Messiah.

Chapter Fourteen
Of Miscellany

Like a meandering stream, we are now going to wander through the Hebrew Scriptures, unearthing little gems along the way. We start with a fascinating little snippet, a piece of visual word play that is totally missed by every Bible translation. It is even missed by those reading the Bible in its original Hebrew. The only place you'll be able to see this is by looking at a *Torah* scroll and, even then, it will have to be one in the *ashkenazi* (northern Europe) tradition. It's near the end of the Exodus story, at the parting of the Red Sea for the Israelites.

> *When Pharaoh's horses, chariots and horsemen went into the sea, the* LORD *brought the waters of the sea back over them, but the Israelites walked through the sea on dry ground* (Exodus 15:19).

To be more specific, it's the second half of the verse that's of interest, translated as follows in the Jewish tradition, "*the sea, and the Israelites walked on the dry land in the midst of the sea*". In Hebrew it appears on the scroll exactly as follows:

הים   ובני ישראל הלכו ביבשה בתוך   הים

Two identical words are right-justified and left-justified. They are the word for "sea" and the point made is to show the Israelites walking in the middle (on dry land), with the sea either side of them. It's a visual thing and so consistent with the whole ethos of the Hebrew language as a *visual* language.

Has that whetted your appetite? Here's another little visual gem. In fact it's just one example of many others that are dotted all over the Hebrew Scriptures. These are the mainstay of the cleaner variety of stand-up comedians. I am talking about *puns* here. There's a nice pun in Isaiah, but you only get it if you're reading it in Hebrew. Here's the English, first of all:

> *The vineyard of the* LORD *Almighty is the house of Israel, and the men of Judah are the garden of his delight. And he looked for justice, but saw bloodshed; for righteousness, but heard cries of distress* (Isaiah 5:7).

It comes at the end of a poem, the allegory of the vineyard. Let's look at the second half of this verse in Hebrew.

למשפט והנה משפח לצדקה והנה צעקה

There it is, don't you get it! Of course you don't, neither would I if it weren't for my reference material. I will repeat it, with phonetics and translation:

למשפט – l'mishpat – for justice
והנה – v'hineh – he looked
משפח – mispach – bloodshed
לצדקה – l'tzedekah – for righteousness
והנה – v'hineh – he looked
צעקה – tz'acha – pain

Can you see it now? See how similar the contrasting words are for justice/bloodshed and for righteousness/pain. It is surely worth further study to see why these disparate words share the same root letters. Sadly, there is not space to do it here, but perhaps you should get hold of a good Biblical Hebrew dictionary and do it yourself. You only see it in the Hebrew, a translation misses it entirely. There are loads of these puns and word plays throughout Hebrew Scripture. You will have to find them yourself ☺.

Here's another visual study that will interest you. You may be familiar with this Scripture:

> *For this is what the* LORD *Almighty says: "After he has honoured me and has sent me against the nations that have plundered you – for whoever touches you touches the apple of his eye"* (Zechariah 2:8).

We use this expression as a warning to those who come against Israel or the Jewish people, but we also use it in more general terms to indicate a favourite, as in *you really love that kid, he's the apple of your eye isn't he?* It's an expression we use without thinking because, let's face it, if we really think about it, *it doesn't make sense.* At least it doesn't in the English translation, but what about the original Hebrew? Well actually, there are three other places in Scripture where this expression can be found (Deuteronomy 32:10, Psalm 17:8 and Proverbs 7:2), but, in each case, the Hebrew is slightly different to that in Zechariah 2:8. In all of these four cases we have:

אישׁון עין *(aleph – yod – shin – vav – Nun   ayin – yod – Nun)* = *ayshown ayin* = apple of your eye.

The second word, *ayin*, takes the same sound as its first letter, ע, and always takes the meaning of "eye", as we saw earlier. (You can also refer to the Appendix.) The first word is far more interesting. It is based on the root word:

אישׁ *(aleph – yod – shin)* = *aysh* = man.

The suffix extends the meaning to "little man". So, the literal meaning of the expression אישׁון עין is, *little man of your eye*, colloquially called the *apple* of your eye. Very strange indeed, that is until you look someone full in the eye. The front dark bit of the eye is called the *pupil* and in the pupil you will see a reflection of yourself, *a little man*! Indeed, the very word *pupil* comes from the Latin word "papilla" and means a "little doll".

What a marvellous image (in both senses). If you look at God, you will see Israel reflected in his eye – that's *one in the eye* for all those who state that God has rejected Israel and the Jews! Interestingly, as I've already said, the Hebrew translates differently in the most famous use of this expression, in Zechariah 2:8:

בבה עין *(bet – vet – hay   ayin – yod – Nun) = bavah ayin = ?*

This is not a straightforward translation; it literally means "the hollow of his eye" and it's just a more scientific way of looking at "the apple of his eye", seeing the eye socket as a hollow opening full of liquid acting as a reflective surface. Jews have always been scientifically minded, even in those days! Again we are shown the descriptive powers of Hebrew, describing the intangible (the great love of God for his people) in the tangible and mundane (the reflection of a person in someone else's eyes).

Away from the visual now and into a study that demonstrates the difference between the Greek and Hebraic world views, the worldly and the biblical mindsets. Sometimes a passage is translated with such a subtle change in emphasis that the reader misses out on the fact that what we are reading has been tweaked to be consistent with our modern world view. Such a passage is Exodus 24:7:

> *Then he took the Book of the Covenant and read it to the people. They responded, "We will do everything the* LORD *has said; we will obey."*

This seems straightforward enough. Here are the Israelites responding positively to Moses reading from the "book of the Law" that he had written at God's instigation. They *heard* his words, then they promised to *do what they say*, to obey them. This is how we do things. We listen, we mull over what we've just heard, then we respond. The only thing is … this is not what the Hebrew words say. The key words are right at the end of the verse:

נעשה ונשמע *(nun – ayin – sin – hey   vav – nun – shin – mem – ayin)* = na'aseh v'nishma.

This translates literally as "we will do and we will hear". You may have detected a familiar root in the second word – the word is *shema* (שמע) – that we looked at in an earlier chapter, when we considered Deuteronomy 6:4 (Hear O Israel, the LORD our God, the LORD is one).

How is this possible? Surely it's the wrong way round? We hear first ... and *then* we do! Yes, that's true in our "Greek", Western world view. That's how we process information – we listen, we analyse and try to understand what has been said, then we act. This is *not* the Hebraic way. In the Hebraic world view, God instructs us and we obey. It is not necessary for us to mull things over or understand his words, we just *do what he asks*. He doesn't instruct us in order that we may understand him:

> *"For my thoughts are not your thoughts, neither are your ways my ways," declares the* LORD (Isaiah 55:8).

No, instead he instructs us *in order that we may live!* Understanding comes from obedience to his commands, although it may take a lifetime for it to sink into our stubborn hearts! How many people have made understanding a stumbling block to making a leap of faith? How many people do you know who would say something like this: *"How can I believe in the Bible when it doesn't explain to my satisfaction where Cain's wife came from?"* Or, *"How can I believe in a God who allows innocent babies to die?"*

There are some Bible verses that just roll off the tongue and, in fact, become clichés that we drag out to prove a point. One such verse is Zechariah 4:6:

> *So he said to me, "This is the word of the* LORD *to Zerubbabel: 'Not by might nor by power, but by my Spirit,' says the* LORD *Almighty.*

Our general understanding of this is that we should not depend on our strength, our might, our power. It provides a contrast between our ways and God's ways. No, I'm not about to debunk this, rest assured, but it is useful to explore the original Hebrew, especially after all we have learned about the inadequacies of English in translating some Hebrew words or concepts. The word translated as "might" here is the following:

בְּחַיִל *(vet – chet – yod – lamed)* = *v'chayil* = by might.

It's *not* the same word translated as "strength" in this other well-known verse:

> *Love the* LORD *your God with all your heart and with all your soul and with all your strength* (Deuteronomy 6:5).

מְעֹד *(mem – ayin – dalet)* = *me'od* = strength, might, force.

This word is very much connected with physical strength and prowess, but the word in Zechariah 4:6, *v'chayil*, is more far-reaching. It also refers to wealth, influence, or valour and is concerned with outward expressions of your power, rather than just the size of your muscles. What we should learn from this is that the world's way of leadership, the physical trappings of power and wealth, just don't "cut the mustard" with God. Sadly, so many Christian leaders just don't see this and follow the world's model of flaunting the trappings of power and wealth. Haven't we heard this before – *"Look, I need this private jet, that way I can minister to my flock more efficiently"?*

> *Not so with you. Instead, whoever wants to become great among you must be your servant* (Matthew 20:26).

Let's be people of humility, true servants, rather than flaunting our *chayil*.

The book of Numbers is not usually recognised as a source of great narrative enjoyment, but there's one story there that catches the eye, from Numbers 22 onwards. It's the story of Balaam, he of the talking ass. It's a story of two Gentiles who wanted to do wrong to the Hebrews, a king and a prophet. The king was Balak, the Moabite:

Now Balak son of Zippor saw all that Israel had done to the Amorites (Numbers 22:2).

We have already learned that Hebrew names have insightful meanings. So. ...

בלק *(bet – lamed – Khaph)* = **Balak** = destroyer.
צפור *(tsade – pey – pey – vav – resh)* = **Zippor** = little bird, sparrow.

So we have *Destroyer*, son of *Little Bird*. An interesting start. Birds were associated with the supernatural and it was going to be by *divination* that the Hebrews were going to be supposedly destroyed. There was a Jewish tradition that Balak himself had used a magical metallic bird for divination purposes. But this time he called upon someone else, Balaam:

... sent messengers to summon Balaam son of Beor, who was at Pethor, near the River, in his native land (Numbers 22:5).

Again we have two names:

בלעם *(bet – lamed – ayin – Mem)* = **Balaam** = swallower of a nation.
בעור *(bet – ayin – vav – resh)* = **Beor** = blaze, burning.

This time we have *Swallower of a Nation, son of a burning*. Interesting? Confusing? Well this was an interesting man. He had sufficient knowledge of God to use his sacred name (יהוה) and even to speak to him, and supposedly had the power to bless and curse people.

> *"Spend the night here," Balaam said to them, "and I will bring you back the answer the* LORD *gives me." So the Moabite princes stayed with him* (Numbers 22:8).

Perhaps being *son of a burning* was an allusion to Moses meeting God at the burning bush, so perhaps there was a time before Balaam had turned to the darker side. What was Balaam now? Supposedly a prophet, he was never called one, but he was given a title:

> *In addition to those slain in battle, the Israelites had put to the sword Balaam son of Beor, who practised divination* (Joshua 13:22).

He was a diviner, a practice denounced by Moses in Deuteronomy 18:14. He was also some kind of mystic, who fell into a prostrate state while he was having visions, as he self-declared in Numbers 24:4. He really seemed like a good guy gone bad. Yet God was still able to use him. In fact, wasn't it through the mouth of Balaam that we read the following?

> *"I see him, but not now; I behold him, but not near. A star will come out of Jacob; a sceptre will rise out of Israel. He will crush the foreheads of Moab, the skulls of all the sons of Sheth. Edom will be conquered; Seir, his enemy, will be conquered, but Israel will grow strong. A ruler will come out of Jacob and destroy the survivors of the city"* (Numbers 24:17–19).

The *son of a burning* here predicts the coming of the Messiah. God will really use *anyone* to get his story out.

There is one method of Bible interpretation that totally encapsulates and represents the *Hebraic* mindset. It's not the traditional Protestant techniques, such as historical-cultural and contextual analysis, as worthy as they are. It is not the mystical approach of meditating, praying and waiting for illumination from the Holy Spirit, as worthy as that is. It certainly ain't asking someone else what a passage means, as worthy as that other person might be. It's a method called *Midrash*. It's what learned rabbis in *yeshivas* – huddled over Hebrew Scripture and a whole gamut of scholarly commentaries – do. It's the locking of intellects fed by lifetimes of study. It's the plucking out of memory and weaving together of Hebrew Scriptures in ways that would leave most of us, trained to think in a totally different way, gasping.

You won't read about *Midrash* in your Christian manuals of hermeneutics, yet the men who God used as his agents to write down his words were trained in it; it was as natural to them as the air that they breathed. It's not one that comes naturally to our Greek educated minds, because we possess neither the building blocks nor the processes to make it work for us. The building blocks are the very words of the Hebrew Scriptures – all of them, memorised and understood in context. Yes, many of us possess a reasonably comprehensive knowledge of the *Tenach*, but every word ... and in context? Let's get real here!

As for the processes, it's an ability to find connections between these building blocks, in ways that can sometimes boggle the mind. It can involve phrases, words, even single letters, and to our "Greek" minds can seem illogical, even random. That's its beauty ... it's so un-Greek! Before we see an example of this, let's look at the word itself.

מדרש *(mem – dalet – resh – shin)* = **Midrash** = story, investigate, study.

It is taken from a verb:

דרש *(dalet – resh – shin)* = **drash** = to seek, study, inquire.

Here's an example. It's not an easy one – I can barely get my brain around it – but it's been included just to show you how the Hebraic mind can work. This is taken from a *Midrash* written some time ago, called *Tanhuma Noah 11*.

[God said to Noah] "Come out of the ark." David said, "Free my soul from prison." When Noah was in the ark, he prayed constantly, "Free my soul from prison," as it is said, "Therefore let every faithful man pray to You, in a time when You may be found, that the rushing mighty waters [shetef mayim rabbim] not overtake him" [Psalm 32:6]. God said to Noah, "It is decreed before Me that you shall not leave this prison [closed condition] till twelve months are up." So we find in Isaiah 49:8, "in an hour of favour I answer you . . . saying to the prisoners, 'Go free.'" For they [the people of the ark] were forbidden [lit.imprisoned] to have sexual relations. Why? Because when the world is in trouble and destruction, human beings are forbidden to procreate; so that there should not be a situation in which man is building while God is destroying.

Yes, it means little to us, but what was happening between the rabbis who created this little vignette was that they were connecting up Scriptures from the Genesis Flood story, Psalms and Isaiah, linked very tenuously on ideas of freeing the soul and praying through adversity. Yes, there is much speculation here, but the raw material is God's Word and the end result is only there as a conversation starter. The point is to get us talking and thinking about God, not to win an argument or score points off each other, or even have a definitive answer to a theological question. It's the connecting up of Scriptures written at different times, by different people with different contexts, but with the understanding that there is only one author, God himself, so these considerations just fade away. This is *Midrash* and perhaps the essence of it is the journey and not the destination. Perhaps it would be best now to go through a *Midrash* that we could all understand, so that we can appreciate what we've all been missing. Let's look at Numbers 7:42–43:

On the sixth day Eliasaph son of Deuel, the leader of the people of Gad, brought his offering. His offering was one silver plate weighing a hundred and thirty shekels, and one

*silver sprinkling bowl weighing seventy shekels, both accord-
ing to the sanctuary shekel, each filled with fine flour mixed
with oil as a grain offering. ...*

This was the dedication ceremony for the portable Tabernacle
in the desert. This short passage describes the gifts brought by
Eliasaph, one of the tribal leaders. A small passage, but so much
to dissect. Firstly, from the Midrash commentary in *Numbers
Rabbah 13, 20*:

> **One silver basin.** *This was Moses who was thrown into the
> Nile. Another interpretation: He was thrown out of Egypt,
> as it says, "Moses fled..." (Exodus 2:15).* **70 shekels by the
> sanctuary weight.** *These are the 70 elders, all of whom
> Moses counted as prophets from what the Holy One, praise
> is He, said to him, "then you shall go with the elders of Israel
> to the king..." (Exodus 3:18). And it similarly says, "Gather
> for me seventy of Israel's elders..." (Numbers 11:16).* **Both
> filled with choice flour with oil mixed for a meal offering.**
> *He and they were all filled with the Holy Spirit, and they
> were filled with the Holy Spirit from Moses, and Moses
> was not diminished at all. A person lights one candle from
> another; the candle is lit while the other is not diminished.
> A person who smells an etrog benefits and the etrog is not
> diminished at all.*

What can we make from this then? Well the gift was a silver plate
weighing 130 shekels and a silver bowl weighing 70 shekels. The
shekel is now a coin, but in those days it came from a root word
meaning "to weigh". What's all this about Moses and the silver
basin? What's the connection here? It's actually Hebrew word
play. Here's the Hebrew word used here for basin:

מזרק *(mem – zayin – resh – Khaph)* = *mizrak*.

They noticed that it is similar to this word:

זרק *(zayin – resh – Khaph)* = *zarak.*

This word means "to throw" and it is the root word for *basin*, in the sense that potters *throw* the clay onto the potter's wheel. So here we have Moses accepting a gift that reminded him of being "thrown" into the Nile when he was a child. It could also have reminded him of when he was "thrown" out of Egypt, after he killed the Egyptian (Exodus 2:15).

The details of the weights and materials in this passage all have their interpretations, too. The silver could also hark back to Moses' early childhood, in fact to his parents. Again it's a word play:

כסף *(khaph – samech – Phey)* = *kesef* = silver.

כסופין *(khaph – samech – vav – phey – yod – Nun)* = *kisufin* = longing.

The *silver* alludes to the "longing" of Moses' parents when he was consigned to the Nile. The 130 shekels alludes (according to some) to the number of years from the descent to Egypt by the Israelites to the birth of Moses. The 70 shekels allude to the 70 elders whom Moses was asked to appoint over the Israelites (Numbers 11). Finally, there was another word play:

אחת *(aleph – chet – tav)* = *echad* = one (as in *one* silver plate or silver bowl).
אחות *(aleph – chet – vav – tav)* = *echot* = sister (as in *Miriam*, who saved Moses).

Lots of connections, and most are not the connections *we* would make. There are more. The rabbis took the words "each filled", referring to the plate and the bowl and applied it to these 70 elders *and* Moses. They asserted that Moses lost none of his anointing when he gave the Holy Spirit to the elders (Numbers 11:16–17) and gave a couple of experiences from everyday life to back this up: a candle doesn't lose its flame when it lights another, and when one smells an *etrog* (citrus fruit), the fruit is not diminished.

Then we can apply this Midrash to ourselves. When we give to others, as Moses did to the 70 elders, we can benefit too, as Moses did ultimately with the help they eventually provided for him. By lighting the flame in others, it can serve to keep the flame burning in ourselves. Moses gave a *spiritual* gift to others, as Eliasaph gave a *practical* gift to the Tabernacle. It is better to give than to receive.

All this from that short passage in Numbers, something that would undoubtedly pass unnoticed in our own study as we ploughed through the book and its pesky ... numbers! And that's Midrash. There's something wonderful here that we Christians are missing. How many *Messianic* Midrashim (plural of "Midrash") will pour out from the yeshivas once the Holy Spirit hits them and they confess *Yeshua* as their Messiah? We will have to be patient and wait.

And finally.... I've always been impressed when I hear that great blessing, *the Aaronic Blessing*, recited in Hebrew. It has an air of majesty about it, I've always thought. So, how about if we try to learn it, as it is not too long? And how about, while we are doing so, we find out *exactly* what it means? In Bible times the chanting of this prayer was indeed an awesome occasion. When the priests prayed this, it was said that the divine Presence would shine on their fingers and no-one was allowed to look, out of respect for God. Even today, Orthodox Jews will look to the ground when chanting this blessing. Here it is in English:

> *The LORD bless you and keep you; the LORD make his face shine upon you and be gracious to you; the LORD turn his face toward you and give you peace* (Numbers 6:24–26).

And in Hebrew:

אליך פניו יהוה יאר וישמרך יהוה יברכך

eleycha	panav	Adonai	ya'er	v'yishmerecha	Adonai	y'varecha
to you	His face	May The LORD shine		and keep you	May The LORD	bless you

שלום לך וישם אליך פניו יהוה ישא ויחנך

shalom	lecha	v'yasem	eleycha	panav	Adonai	yisa	vichunecha
peace	to you	and give	to you	May the LORD lift up His face and be gracious to you			

Practise this a few times (remember, from right to left) and then we'll move on.

The third word, וישמרך (v'yishmerecha) is from the root שמר (shamar), with the meaning of guarding or protecting, as with a shepherd and his flocks.

The fourth word, יאר (ya'er) is from אור, with the understanding of bringing order, as light shines in the dark.

The sixth (and eleventh) word, פיו (panav) is from פנים (paniym), with the meaning of a face, reflecting the inner essence of the individual.

The eighth word, ויחנך (vichunecha) is from the root חנן (chanan), with an understanding that graciousness is not just an outward appearance but an inner virtue, connected with love, friendship and community.

And of course the final word, שלם (shalom) is best understood as completeness and wholeness.

So this blessing could be more clumsily, but certainly more evocatively, expressed thus:

> The LORD will bless you and he will put a guard around you. The LORD will shine from his very being to you. The LORD will provide you with sincere love and friendship and provide you with completeness and wholeness.

I sincerely hope that this book has also been a blessing for you. We are now going to finish with a vignette built around a detective story that encapsulates much that you should have learned in this book. Enjoy.

Chapter Fifteen
Of Mysteries

If you were to ask a Christian what Psalm speaks most of Messiah Jesus, particularly in the context of his crucifixion, the answer would invariably be Psalm 22. Here are the first fifteen verses:

My God, my God, why have you forsaken me?
Why are you so far from saving me,
so far from the words of my groaning?
O my God, I cry out by day, but you do not answer,
by night, and am not silent.
Yet you are enthroned as the Holy One;
you are the praise of Israel.
In you our fathers put their trust;
they trusted and you delivered them.
They cried to you and were saved;
in you they trusted and were not disappointed.
But I am a worm and not a man,
scorned by men and despised by the people.
All who see me mock me;
they hurl insults, shaking their heads:
"He trusts in the LORD; *let the* LORD *rescue him.*
Let him deliver him, since he delights in him."
Yet you brought me out of the womb;
you made me trust in you even at my mother's breast.
From birth I was cast upon you;
from my mother's womb you have been my God.
Do not be far from me,
for trouble is near and there is no one to help.

Many bulls surround me;
strong bulls of Bashan encircle me.
Roaring lions tearing their prey open their mouths wide
*   against me.*
I am poured out like water, and all my bones are out of
*   joint.*
My heart has turned to wax; it has melted away within me.
My strength is dried up like a potsherd,
and my tongue sticks to the roof of my mouth;
you lay me in the dust of death."

It's the very next verse that I want us to explore now.
   Here's the NIV translation of Psalm 22:16:

Dogs have surrounded me;
a band of evil men has encircled me,
they have pierced my hands and my feet.

Christians have marvelled at these words for over two thousand years, giving a graphic fore-telling of Jesus' agonies on the cross at Calvary. But are they correct? The Jewish Bible certainly doesn't believe so. Here is their most common translation of that verse.

"For dogs have encompassed me: a company of evil-doers
have inclosed me; **like a lion, they are at my hands and my**
feet." (JPS translation from Masoretic text).

You can see the difference and you can understand their perceived reasons for doing what they did, but surely they have taken great liberties with the text, haven't they? There was only one thing to do to settle this mystery. What does the original Hebrew text say? What does the Masoretic text say? Did it *really* say what was reported by the JPS translation in 1917?
   What has happened to the word *lion*? Why is it not translated in the KJV and the NIV and no doubt all of the other Christian translations? This worried me quite a lot. Then I searched the

web and discovered that it worries a lot of people. So I couldn't just leave it at that! Here is the relevant section, the part that can either be *they have pierced my hands and my feet* or *like a lion they are at my hands and my feet*.

Here is the Masoretic text: (due to slippage this is actually verse 17, rather than verse 16):

ורגלי	ידי	כארי
And my feet	my hands	like a lion

Well that's that then, the Christians are wrong … aren't they?

Here's a (back) translation of the Septuagint Greek for that verse, put back into Hebrew.

ורגלי	ידי	כארו
And my feet	my hands	they pierced

Spot the difference? You can see it's down to one letter. In the first word, the Masoretic text has a *yod* (י) as its final letter, whereas the Septuagint has a *vav* (ו) as its final letter. So it appears that, with the source material available to the *Masoretes*, the final letter appeared to be a *yod*, but with that available to the Septuagint translators, it appeared to be a *vav*. Which is it to be, *yod* or *vav*? Before we discuss this, there are other considerations, for both sets of scribes/translators.

The *Masoretes* had a problem. Firstly the passage had no verb, meaning that its meaning was a bit forced and strangled i.e. it wasn't very good Hebrew. Secondly, the Hebrew word for *lion* used is subtly different to the word used in two other verses of the same Psalm (verses 14 and 22 in Masoretic text), so why was a different word used here in verse 17? And, thirdly, who's ever heard of a lion 'surrounding the feet' of their prey? They go straight for the throat, don't they? It just doesn't make sense.

The Septuagint translators also had a problem. The Hebrew word כארו didn't actually appear anywhere else in Scripture but was similar to the root word (כרה) that gave the meaning of "to dig", which is not *exactly* the same as the word that future translators ended up with i.e. "to pierce".

So we are faced possibly with the same dilemma in both cases. A cynical observer would say that each had an agenda. The Masoretes, belonging to a people (the Jews) hounded, rejected and persecuted by Christians, were in a tempting position of scoring a minor victory against their adversaries, in the form of the translation of a foundational Scripture that renders a key prophecy worthless. The Christian translators (who used the Septuagint as well as the Masoretic text) had to decide between the two. Would objectivity go out of the window when choosing between two alternative meanings, when one of them seemed to be speaking of the crucifixion ... but not exactly?

Back to the Masoretes. The absence of a verb was a problem, exacerbated by their decision to put a punctuation mark after the first half of the verse, acting as a semi-colon and isolating the phrase we are looking at. So a verb was glaring in its omission. One was added in the Aramaic paraphrase (*targum*) of this verse, which states "(they bite) like a lion", but that is not relevant to our argument as we are concentrating solely on the Hebrew letters.

The early Christian translators followed the gist of the Septuagint and ended up with variations of the word "to dig". Jerome in his Vulgate, actually came up with two possible translations "they have dug ..." and "they have bound ...." By the time we get to the English translators, the accepted usage was "to pierce", as it was judged to be the best word to use in the context of the verse, "dogs have surrounded me ...", with the image of a pack of wild hounds tearing at the flesh of their prey. Also they alluded to Psalm 40:6:

> *Sacrifice and offering you did not desire, but my ears you have pierced; burnt offerings and sin offerings you did not require.*

So we have seen the two positions. What about the evidence? Now it gets interesting. When the Dead Sea Scrolls were discovered, one set found were the *Psalms scrolls*, thirty-nine manuscripts in all, including extracts from Psalm 22. As these manuscripts would predate both the Masoretic text and Septuagint, could the problem of the "yod or vav" be solved? Sadly, no – the manuscript was damaged just at the very point where verse 16 would have been!

Then, in 1953, another discovery was made in the Dead Sea area. It was at Nahal Hever where they found a scrap of Psalm 22, which included verse 16.The writing was faint and a magnifying glass was needed. What did they see? Was it a *yod* or a *vav*? This is what they found:

כארו ידי ורגלי

It was a *vav*! It was a "piercing" *not* a "lion"! Further confirmation was that the first letter of the next word in the text was a *yod* and it looked *nothing* like this vav! This manuscript dated back to the first century, a thousand years before the Masoretes and even earlier than much of the Septuagint. Now a *vav* and a *yod* are similar and one could countenance the possibility that, on the manuscript available to the Masoretes, the stem of the *vav* could have just faded. Or it could have been – "God forbid" – a scribal error on the original manuscript.

But now we have to go back to motivations and agendas. We already saw that the Christian translators into English, from the "King James" people to almost modern times, had both versions at their disposal, without the Nahal Hever discovery, and *all of them* went with the version that spoke into their faith view, with a messianic prophecy of Jesus on the cross.

So, to the collective relief of Christians everywhere, the King James Version actually got it right in this case. Of course, the people at the Jewish Publication Society have their agenda to follow so it will be interesting to see if they modify their translation in the light of this new evidence! They made an editorial decision and one can only wonder if modern Christian translators would have modified their "Old Testament" if that Hebrew letter had been a *yod*!

The Jewish translators certainly didn't; they still consider the Masoretic text 100% reliable and so no changes have been made. Yet the Masoretes, despite their reputation, scholarship and legendary accuracy, actually got it wrong here either because of a tiny, tiny mistake of a *Sopher* or because of the smallest aberration on the manuscript from which they copied. Some blinkered folk have even cynically suggested that the Masoretes have been found out here tampering with the text. If so, then they did a real amateur job of it, creating a distinctly dodgy, ungrammatical and uncontextual piece of work. Any student of the *Masorah* would know that these master scribes were not only the best at what they did but mindful of the curses attached to tampering with God's Word. We have to put this down to an honest mistake by a fallible human being. It doesn't mean that we can't trust the Masoretic text but it does show the need for other texts for corroboration, especially when there is so much at stake. The Septuagint may have had a chequered history and it is certainly not favoured by most biblical scholars (because it is a translation rather than a copy in the original language), but it got it right in this case. The hand of God could be seen in this important episode, in the timely discovery of the psalm parchment, to settle the argument once and for all.

We need to know of other such cases because it is far more important to know *what God's words are* than *our* interpretation. When Jesus was on the cross, he uttered these words:

> *About the ninth hour Jesus cried out in a loud voice, "Eloi, Eloi, lama sabachthani?" –which means, "My God, my God, why have you forsaken me?" (Matthew 27:46).*

The subtext here was that, in one of his final declarations, he was in fact saying: *Psalm 22, Psalm 22!* The words he was using were the opening words of the Psalm, a device used by Jews to identify the complete passage in question. Reading the opening words was like reading the title of a piece of Scripture. Jesus, like all educated Jews of his day, knew every word of Psalm 22 and he also knew that here he was fulfilling it, especially v. 16. How many of today's Christians would have made that same connection? This demonstrates the importance of the Hebrew Scriptures, the sadly neglected "Old Testament", the *back story* to everything Jesus did and stood for in his brief time on earth.

Chapter Sixteen

God's Signature

When we were created in God's image, I imagine it being as though he signed us off with a flourish of his divine fountain pen, leant back on his divine chair and then watched the ink smudge as we began to mess it up! Adam fell from grace and opted for a life in which he thought he would have knowledge that would put him in charge, rather than hooking up daily with the Creator, the *source* of all wisdom, whom he had known in those walks in the garden.

It was all downhill from there. I offered a rationale for it in my book *To Life*. I suggest that perhaps a Hebraic, "God-centred", mindset was the default before Adam sinned and the "Greek", "man-centred" mindset became the default after he sinned. You can't deny that the focus did shift from God to man as a result of the Fall. The original state found Adam and Eve in communion with God, following his instructions and living in a God-created paradise. The fallen state, however, saw Adam and Eve acting on their own initiative, disobeying God and forced to leave this paradise and create a life for themselves. This is what we have inherited, and perhaps it is fair to say that, despite all the scientific progress that man has made, our yearning is nothing more than to return to the simplicity and connectedness of the Garden of Eden. I contend that this is the goal of the "Hebraic" mindset.

The "Hebraic" mindset? What's this got to do with Hebrew ... and the Hebrews? It's all connected, because it's all part of God's plan and he knows exactly what he's doing. It was all about communicating this plan to all of mankind and the first thing he did was to put a medium of communication into place, a language that bore his signature: *Hebrew*. He then identified a people, a nation not yet born but living within the seed of one man, Abraham. Here was a righteous man, perhaps the most godly since Noah, a man who listened to God and carried out his plans, as strange or terrible as they may have seemed at the time. This seed carried within it a divine blessing:

> *The LORD had said to Abram, "Leave your country, your people and your father's household and go to the land I will show you.*
>
> *"I will make you into a great nation and I will bless you; I will make your name great, and you will be a blessing. I will bless those who bless you, and whoever curses you I will curse; and all peoples on earth will be blessed through you"* (Genesis 12:1–4).

As the seed grew and flourished, a nation was born that carried God's signature, the Hebrews – fallible people like others yet blessed with a unique calling. Their history spans the whole "Old Testament", from the above verse to the end. These were the people of the seed, whose triumphs, achievements, weaknesses and disasters were written down, through divine inspiration, as the *Hebrew Scriptures*, the Word of God in the language of God, Hebrew. From this Word of God we are able to glimpse the functioning of the *Hebraic mindset*, reflected in the words and actions of the Hebrew people. And we have found that only the Hebrew language is equipped for us to do this. The penny will drop as we discover exactly what the *Hebraic* mindset is. In my book *To Life*, I defined it thus:

- Putting God at the centre of what we do.
- Exercising faith in God.
- Actions resulting from this faith.

It can also be summarised in one sentence: *unswerving faith in God and his Word and our unconditional response of obedience to him in our thoughts, lives, words and deeds.* This, of course, ought to be the default *Christian* mindset. But, if we are honest, the witness of two thousand years of the church has often fallen far short of this.

So why were the Hebrews set apart as an example of this? Surely they messed up, even ending up in exile as a result of *not* demonstrating unswerving faith in God, etc. This is true, but what about the men and women of character, those prophets, priests and patriarchs (and the odd king) who inhabit the pages of Scripture and whose stories instruct and inspire us? They are the ones who demonstrate the "Hebraic mindset" through their complete faith in God and their response to him in their thoughts, lives and deeds. They are the ones we are to follow, the rest are ... too much like us!

The Hebrew Scriptures show us a parallel narrative of God reaching out to his people and the outworking of his people's responses. The history of the Jewish people within God's Word is no ordinary history; it is an account of the interactions between God and man. No other ancient people could boast of such a history. Their narratives were full of the processes of nature, harvest, death, fertility and annual cycles rather than a single, wonderful, complex, breathtaking love story of God, and his (mainly) unrequited love for his Creation. This is the core story and everything else is incidental, even events of cosmic significance as the Creation of everything else in the universe, from the moon and the stars, to the fish and the tumbleweed.

It's all about us, it really is ... but only from *his* perspective, which is why we must be Hebraic in our thoughts and deeds, to see it all from *his* point of view.

> LORD, *you have been our dwelling place throughout all generations* (Psalm 90:1).

We now turn our focus back on the Hebrew language and again ask why God chose it (or created it) as the language to communicate to his people and, effectively, to everyone else too, all those who are willing to train themselves to learn the language.

We have discovered four good reasons why God chose Hebrew as his language of revelation.

• Because every letter can add a *visual meaning*.

Hebrew evolved from a picture language and, if you have some ideas of these original pictures, then each Hebrew letter can speak to you. For example, the aleph (א) would suggest an authority figure and the bet (ב) is associated with a house or tent. Bringing these two letters together give us the word *av* (אב), the word for "father", the authority figure in the home.

• Because every word can have such a *depth of meaning*.

We learned that Hebrew words tend to be constructed around a 3-letter root system. This means that knowledge of the key roots used in the Hebrew Scriptures can give you a fresh understanding of God's Word, particularly when you start to see connections between words that you didn't notice before. For example, the following three words all share the same root: amen (אמן), emet (אמת), meaning "truth" and emunah (אמונה), meaning "trust". The connection between them is plain to see in the Hebrew as well as the English translation.

• Because it is a language of *action*.

The Hebraic mindset is characterised by actions flowing from God's Word cementing to your heart. It is therefore not surprising that Hebrew, with its accent on verbs rather than nouns, is ideally constructed to deal with this.

• Because it is a *language of the senses* with simple vivid words and a direct simplicity, drawing the spiritual from the mundane.

Hebrew is a very earthy and practical language, using earthy words to convey intangible things, such as emotions. For example we saw that it was noticed that when one gets angry, the nostrils begin to flare and redden. So the Hebrew word for "anger" (אַף) is also the word for "nose".

So, to recap, we can now appreciate the wonderful provision God made for us in supplying the perfect language to do the job. This was the language (or at least an earlier form of it) that his finger used to carve out the "Ten Commandments" on those tablets of stone that Moses brought down with him from Mount Sinai, after receiving the rest of the teachings of the *Torah*, which he wrote down himself. With a few additions by Joshua, his successor, this became "The Book of the Law", stored in the holiest places, first in the portable Tabernacle, then in Solomon's Temple.

But when the times of Moses and Joshua gave way to the Judges, then the Kings, this book became less and less a part of the corporate life of the Hebrews. The evidence was in the decline in public standards and behaviour, in the infiltration of pagan ideas from the nations that surrounded them, things that would have been deemed detestable and worthy of great punishment, if the words of "The Book of the Law" had been heeded, or even known.

Once the Kingdom split in two, the Northern Kingdom, Israel, had reached the point of no return, the actions of the Kings and their subjects inconsistent with their remaining in the land of promise, as decreed by the unread judgements in the book. Then came a brief respite as "The Book of the Law" was re-discovered by King Josiah and the kingdom was swept clean of the pagan filth. But too late, as first Israel dropped into the black hole of history, then Judah was exiled to Babylon.

Seventy years later, the great priest and scribe Ezra, the custodian of "The Book of the Law" in exile, brought its teachings back to the land and re-launched the Hebrews as the People of the Book, which now started to include the other writings, histories, prophecies and poetry that would eventually be recognised as the Hebrew Scriptures. Ezra and the men of the Great Assembly began to organise the meticulous copying of these Scriptures by *Sopherim*, the dedicated band of scribes, initiating an unbroken chain leading right up to modern times. They worked from the source material of the original documents held in the Temple, ensuring that God's Word was going to be transmitted as accurately as was humanly possible.

In the meantime, other documents, perhaps not as accurate as these, were used to produce the *Septuagint*, the translation of the Hebrew Scriptures into Greek. This was a somewhat flawed translation, but not without some worth, and was the "Bible" of the early Christians, who welcomed a Greek version of the "Old Testament", though later generations of Jews rejected it.

Others mistakenly saw the Septuagint as an "inspired" translation, as did some later concerning the King James Version. Other translations include Jerome's *Latin Vulgate*, much beloved of the Catholics, who made heavy use of it in their medieval Bibles, and Origen's *Hexapla*, which included alternative Greek translations alongside that of the Septuagint. Sadly, many Christians at this time were not just reading their Scriptures in Greek but were also interpreting them using a Greek mindset, drawing on the philosophy of such as Plato, reinterpreted by a succession of learned men, mainly in Alexandria, Egypt, from Philo the Jew through to Origen the church Father.

By then, the canon of the Hebrew Scriptures, the *Tenach*, had been fixed, by the Jewish Council in Yavneh, with the Christian "Old Testament" also fixed soon afterwards, with the same Scriptures but re-arranged slightly differently. The Scriptures in the *Tenach* were in consonant form, which was fine before the Jews were dispersed and had a consensual agreement on how to pronounce the words, but by the time we reach the 7th or 8th century AD this had become a problem, with the Jewish population spread throughout the known world.

Along came the *Masoretes*, a dedicated band of scribes who worked together over hundreds of years to produce the definitive Hebrew Scriptures, based on the most accurate sources and resplendent with vowels, accents and cantillation marks, so each word could be spoken aloud and even sung. They were both meticulous and amazingly faithful to God's Word, including a commentary to their work in side margins, footnotes and appendices, to explain the text, particularly when there was any possibility of confusion, or where the Hebrew text was a bit obscure.

All Jewish English translations of the *Tenach* are taken lock, stock and barrel from the Masoretic text, and versions of the Christian English "Old Testament" are based mainly on this text, but also taking into consideration new findings through the Dead Sea Scrolls and also referencing the Septuagint and other translations on problem passages. The King James Version was, of course, the first serious mass-market English translation and, for all its faults, was at least a serious attempt at word-for-word translation. Since then, English translations have increasingly been churned out in the response to the needs of a rapidly-changing world. Of course, it is preferable to have our Bibles in legible modern English, but latterly Bibles have been produced as marketing initiatives, bowing to such "necessities" of political correctness as gender neutrality. These Bibles have mostly been translated according to the rules of *dynamic equivalence*, which pays more attention to the "gist of the passage translated" than the words themselves.

So where are we now? The 64 million dollar question begs to be asked: *Which Bible do we read if we want the most authentic experience?* Which Bible do you recommend? Now there's a question! The easy answer, certainly in terms of the Hebrew Scriptures, is to encourage us all to learn Hebrew (and some Aramaic) and read from the Masoretic text directly, paying heed to the *Masorah* notes (which are mostly in Aramaic). Good answer? No, it isn't, because it simply isn't realistic for most of us, me included. We are stuck with the need for a good English translation, whether we like it or not.

The best I can do is to at least suggest translations that you should avoid for the *authentic* experience and that would be all the paraphrase Bibles and all those with a sociological slant, which are intended to appeal to groups of people who would otherwise not touch a Bible. I personally use an NIV and the NKJV (New King James Version), but would use websites such as *BibleStudyTools* (www.biblestudytools.com) or *Bible*

Gateway (www.biblegateway.com), to make comparisons for any given verses.

The fear I have about paraphrased and stylised Bibles is that the Bible could be seen just as a book full of good stories, just like *Aesop's Fables* or a good anthology of science fiction. Paraphrases might possibly help some to get a *feel* for God's people and get to know God a bit, but aren't you missing out on the *real thing*, God's Word speaking out to the human heart? Is it possible that a reworking of God's Word, even a completely hashed-up reworking of God's Word, can still communicate in the same way? We should never underestimate God's powers to speak to us, but why make it difficult for him? It's bad enough having to depend on fallible (and possibly agenda-ridden) human beings to translate the Hebrew words, but when they are not even translating them but giving us their particular take – often according to their particular theology or world view – isn't that going to obscure God's heart?

And, of course, as this book has hopefully shown you, the further we get away from the pure, evocative simplicity of those individually chosen Hebrew words, the bigger the blessing we miss out on. Here's a verse I quote a lot, but perhaps it's more pertinent in this context than any other place I have used it:

> *I am talking to you Gentiles. Inasmuch as I am the apostle to the Gentiles, I make much of my ministry in the hope that I may somehow arouse my own people to envy and save some of them. For if their rejection is the reconciliation of the world, what will their acceptance be but life from the dead?* (Romans 11:13–15).

I firmly believe that one day there is going to be a stream of Jewish Hebrew scholars pouring out of their *yeshivot*, having discovered *Yeshua* their true Messiah and using their insights from a lifetime of study, to draw out such wonderful truths hidden in those Hebrew words of the *Tenach* that it will be nothing less than *life from the dead*. Perhaps we will find that every Hebrew word in the *Tenach* speaks about Messiah in some way, and we just need the right people to show us the way. These men will show us that *God's signature* is truly written all over his Word and it is just that we have lost the ability to read his handwriting.

But until that time there is plenty of work we can do in getting to know our God a lot better by immersing ourselves in his Word. It's time to get down to business.

Appendix

The Hebrew alphabet

א **aleph** – silent – number 1 = head of ox, leadership, strength.

ב **bet/vet** – b/v – number 2 = tent/house.

ג **gimmel** – g – number 3 = camel, foot.

ד **dalet** – d – number 4 = door, hanging down.

ה **hey** – h – number 5 = man with outstretched arms.

ו **vav** – v – number 6 = tent peg, nail.

ז **zayin** – z – number 7 = weapon.

ח **chet** – ch – number 8 = fence, inside room of house.

ט **tet** – t – number 9 = snake, to surround.

י **yod** – y – number 10 = hand, works, deeds.

כ **kaph/khaph** – ch/k – number 20 / 500 = palm of hand, wing, to open.

ל **lamed** – l – number 30 = shepherd's staff, cattle goad, control.

מ **mem** – m – number 40 / 600 = waves on sea, water.

נ **nun** – n – number 50 / 700 = fish, activity, life.

ס **samech** – s – number 60 = prop, support.

ע **ayin** – silent – number 70 – eye, seeing, understanding.

פ **pey/phey** – ph/p – number 80 / 800 = mouth, speaking.

צ **tsade** – ts – number 90 / 900 = fishhook, man on side.

ק **qoph**– q – number 100 = back of head, sun on horizon.

ר **resh** – r – number 200 = importance, priority.

ש **shin/sin**– sh/s – number 300 = teeth, eating, consuming, destroying.

ת **tav** – t – number 400 = sign, mark.

Recommended reading

Alexander, David & Pat *The Lion Handbook to the Bible* Lion Publishing, 1983.

Benner, Jeff A. *The Ancient Hebrew Language and Alphabet* Virtualbookworm.com 2004.

Berlin, Adele & Brettler Marc, Zvi *The Jewish Study Bible* OUP, 1999.

Brown, Driver, Briggs *Hebrew and English Lexicon* Hendrickson, 2005.

Cohen, Rev. Dr. A *The Soncino Chumash* The Soncino Press Ltd.

Grant, Robert M. & Tracy, David *A Short History of the interpretation of The Bible* Fortress Press, 2005.

Horowitz, Edward *How the Hebrew Language Grew* Ktav, 1988.

Kelley, Page H. & Mynatt, Daniel S. *The Masorah of Biblia Hebraica Stuttgartensia* Eerdmans, 1998.

Maltz, Steve *To Life!* Saffron Planet, 2011.

Moen, Skip *Spiritual Restoration Volume 1* Xulon Press, 2008.

Parsons, John *Zola's Introduction to Hebrew:* Zola Levitt Ministries Inc., 2008.

Phelan, M. W. J. *The Authenticity of English Version Bibles* Twoedged Sword Publications, 2010.

Schenker, Adrian *The Earliest Text of the Hebrew Bible* Society of Biblical Literature, 2003.

Seekins, Dr. Frank T. *Hebrew Word Pictures* Living Word Pictures Inc., 2003.

Tverberg, Lois & Okkema, Bruce *Listening to the Language of the Bible* En-Gedi Resource Center, 2006.

Wheeler, Douglas A. *Hebrew Bible Study Methodology* Calvert Biblical Institute, 2012.

Wurthwein, Ernst *The Text of the Old Testament* Eerdmans, 1995.

By the same author

Available from Amazon, Christian bookshops or directly from
www.sppublishing.com

To Life!
Rediscovering Biblical Church
Have you ever asked the question, where does the world end
and the church begin? Is the 21st century Church truly the best
it could possibly be?

> *"In this fine book, Steve Maltz addresses the issue of religious tradition and its power to force out biblical truth, thus creating disarmed and impotent churches. It is a warning we must heed."* Chris Hill, Bible teacher, writer, broadcaster.

How the Church lost The Way …
… and how it can find it again
The story of how the church has been infiltrated by a pagan virus
that has worked its way through every facet of our Christian life
and how we can start fighting back.

> *"With great insight, explaining many concepts simply, Steve Maltz brings us back to the root of our Christian faith. I believe that every pastor and ordinand in the country will benefit from reading this book."* Mark Weeden, Senior Pastor, Worthing Tabernacle.

How the Church lost The Truth...
... and how it can find it again
What has happened to some key battlegrounds of Christian Truth and how it is that the Church has managed to lose so much that had been revealed to it in the Bible.

> *"I really enjoyed reading it. You are the master of epigrams, full of Jewish wit and humour, which I love. These keep you reading and make the whole interesting. It's so important to add gravy to the meat and you are a good chef. I hope this book will reach those who need it most though I fear they will be irritated, if not infuriated, by your dismissal of so many of their heroes!"* David Pawson (international Bible teacher).

Jesus, the Man of Many Names
A Fresh Understanding from the dawn of time to the End of Days
Are you prepared for a new book about Jesus that does offer fresh insights without boasting new revelations? Drawing on sources from the Jewish world, ancient and modern, the author will take you on an exhilarating, lively and entertaining exploration of the life and times of the Jewish Messiah.

> *"Steve Maltz has a gift for combining pacey writing with crystal-clear distillation of his own careful study of scholarly resources and a firm grip on the gospel. The result is a fascinating new landscape of insight"* David Andrew, Editor, Sword Magazine .

The Truth is out there
The Ultimate World Conspiracy. Who really is pulling the strings?
Is history just a random sequence of events, or are there secret manipulations? What makes us tick? How did the world as we see it come to be? Read this book if you are prepared to be challenged.

Steve Maltz has a rare gift of being able to communicate complex ideas in a way that leaves you thinking that you have read the work of a genius but can still follow his argument clearly. A brilliant read for an evangelist to engage with a sceptic or to give as a gift for "food for thought" Tim Leffler, www.thegoodbookstall.org.uk.

The (other) F-Word
Faith, the Last Taboo

A presentation of the gospel for the modern world. It is direct, uncompromising, engaging and is written to be relevant to the everyday person. Dare you go where modern man fears to tread? You'll either be inspired or provoked, either way it should be an interesting experience.

This is a clear and straightforward evangelistic book, written with real style and panache, and a genuine sense of humour. But at the same time it is serious and God-honouring. I genuinely think that not since C S Lewis have we had a Christian author who has addressed his current generation in such a culture-attuned way. Peter Sammons, author and publisher.

Outcast Nation
Israel, The Jews ... and You

The story of the people and the land through biblical and secular history, tracing the outworkings of God's covenants and offering explanations for both the survival and the success of this outcast nation.

The 'Unavoidable Questions' in the final chapter are particularly challenging, and need to be answered honestly, however uncomfortable they may make you. Highly recommended for reading by as many people as possible, of all beliefs and none. Mary Bartholomew, The Good Bookstall.